Angels of Grace

Angels
of Grace

ANSELM GRUEN

Translated by
DINAH LIVINGSTONE

A Crossroad Book
The Crossroad Publishing Company
New York

First published in the U.S.A. in 1998 by
THE CROSSROAD PUBLISHING COMPANY
370 Lexington Avenue,
New York, NY 10017

First published in Great Britain in 1998 by
BURNS & OATES
Wellwood, North Farm Road,
Tunbridge Wells, Kent TN2 3DR

Original edition *50 Engel für das Jahr*
published by Verlag Herder GmbH & Co. KG
Freiburg, Germany
Copyright © Verlag Herder Freiburg im Breisgau 1997

English translation Copyright © Burns & Oates/
Search Press Limited, 1998

The line drawings are by Penelope Harter, based on Piero
della Francesca; Albrecht Dürer; mosaics in St Mark's,
Venice; the Nuremberg Chronicle (Latin edition, 1493),
and other sources for which the publishers thank the
librarian of Downside Abbey.

Library of Congress Catalog Card Number: 98-72696

ISBN: 0-8245-1761-X

1 2 3 4 5 6 7 8 9 10 03 02 01 00 99 98

Typeset by Search Press Limited
Printed in Finland by Werner Söderström Oy

Contents

Introduction

A young woman is at a New Year's Eve party. This is a circle of people who want to begin the year with a sense of awareness, not just with champagne and fireworks. Someone has written fifty "angels for the year" on fifty cards, and the players are invited to pick themselves an angel for the coming year. Each card has an attitude written on it, representing an approach to life. Of course not all fifty attitudes can determine my life at once. But when I adopt one attitude for a whole year, then that will have an effect on my whole life, something new will happen in me. An attitude can be something to hold on to through life's insecurity. It corresponds to what used to be called a virtue. *Tugend*, the German word for virtue, comes from the verb *taugen*, meaning "to be good for something." So when we exercise a virtue, then our life is good for something, it will succeed. *Virtus*, the Latin word for virtue, means both power and strength. Virtue is a power that can transform our life. The Greek word for virtue was *arete*, meaning the character of a noble and educated person.

The attitudes are related to angels. Today angels have become modern again. For years they held a modest place in theology and the general awareness, but today in countless books they are once again treated with respect. In the Bible angels are God's messengers. They indicate that God is at hand to help and heal. It is not always clear whether they are independent beings, or just images of God's loving and comforting presence. But what is certain is that angels are heralds of another, deeper reality for human beings. We associate them with beautiful images, imaginings and yearnings for another world of security and light, beauty and hope. Part of the deep truth about angels is that they show us there is "more" to our

life, that it relates to something beyond ourselves. Angels are
images of the deep-seated, constant longing for help and healing, which does not come from ourselves. The fact that they
are "in" again today expresses a hope: that our life is not really
empty; it can succeed, we can arrive at our real goal. Angels
are spiritual travelling companions. They bring us into touch
with a desire that each of us has deep down. They are a source
of inspiration. They breathe another, larger life into us, that
goes with this longing in our hearts.

God sends his angels to protect people. In childhood we
were taught the prayer to our guardian angel. Many have given
up the image of a guardian angel. But when they have a lucky
escape from a car accident, they still believe a guardian angel
saved them. It is not important whether it was God himself
who protected us, or an angel sent by him. Images have their
own power. So we can confidently use the language of
images to describe God's helping action. There are angels who
stand by us. Angels watch over us. Angels speak to us in dreams
to tell us which way to go.

Angels are travelling companions. They show us the way, as
once the angel Raphael led young Tobias safely to his desti-
nation. God sends his angel to free Peter from prison, to
strengthen Jesus on the Mount of Olives. Angels often tell us
what we do not understand. An angel tells Mary what will
happen to her. An angel appears to Joseph in a dream to ex-
plain what is going on with Mary, his betrothed. Today angels are back with us again. Rilke often speaks of angels, who
come into our lives. Modern artists paint pictures of angels.
Paul Klee often painted angels in the paintings of his later
years. In 1920 he painted the famous *Angelus Novus*. Marc
Chagall painted the *Angel in Paradise*. Salvador Dali painted
the *Angel*, and there are lots of others. Even pop music has
taken up angels: there are at least five songs titled simply "Angel" (Rod Stewart, Aretha Franklyn, Madonna, Aerosmith,
The Eurythmics), three "Angel of the Morning" (P. P. Arnold,

Juice Newton, Mary Mason); there are "Angel Faces," "Angel Eyes," and "Angel Fingers.". . . Today many people connect the ideas of protection, security, beauty, hope and light with angels.

The Bible says something else about angels. They see God's face. Jesus told us this: "See that you do not despise one of these little ones. For I tell you that in heaven their angels always behold the face of my Father (Matt. 18:10). St Benedict is convinced that monks sing the psalms in the sight of God's angels. They do not sing alone. Angels stand around them and open heaven to their song. Angels bear their prayers to God. They give people hope and confidence that these prayers are not in vain. Angels who stand around us when we pray join heaven and earth. They are beside us, so that we are not here alone praying to God with our troubles. Angels tell us: God is near. You are bathed in his healing and loving presence.

The idea that angels correspond to particular attitudes has been adopted by the Findhorn community. The people in this community are convinced that we can come to an understanding with angels, that angels tell us something about ourselves and our capacity for change. They give us support and imbue us with new attitudes. These are the kind of angels we mean with this book's "fifty angels for the year." They are angels who lead us into attitudes that do us good in our lives.

The angels want to bring out something in us, something we may forget or set aside in our busy everyday lives. It is a beautiful idea to imagine that this year I will be accompanied by the angel of faithfulness or the angel of tenderness, that God sends me an angel who will introduce me into the secret of faithfulness or tenderness. The fifty angels for the year are companions on our life's road. They are messengers of hope that we do not live to no purpose, that we can reach the goal of our life. The fifty attitudes describe powers to shape our life, to transform our life, so that we increasingly match the "original picture": how we could and should be. Angels represent our potential for transformation and calling them angels refers, of course, to the fact that these attitudes are never only the expression of our own efforts. They are also a gift, grace, wisdom given to us.

At the New Year's Eve party, each player drew an angel. They each believed they had picked the very angel they needed for the New Year, to do them good. We could also wish a friend an angel for a birthday or name day. The thoughts we had about an individual angel might help us make our good wishes more concrete. Then the greetings on the card we send will be more than empty words. You can also choose an angel for yourself, to accompany you for the coming week, the coming month or at the New Year.

Choose the angel you need, the one you believe will do you good just now. And if you like you can also swap angels with other people who, you know, also live with one. What has your angel taught you? What experiences have you had with your angel? What new things have happened? What has started moving? What has blossomed in you?

1 The Angel of Love

Love is such an over-used word that I am wary of putting it at the beginning of the list of fifty angels. Pop songs sing about love. Everything revolves around love. Many people connect love with the idea of fulfilled sexuality. But however much the word is abused, in the depths of our heart every one of us longs for love. We want someone to love us unconditionally. We are happy when we fall in love with someone and who returns our love. Then something blossoms inside us. Joy streams from our face. We know we are unconditionally accepted and loved by someone else. Love—as fairy tales tell us—can bring back to life people who have turned to stone. It can turn animals back into human beings. It can make people who are dominated by an instinct (this is the meaning of animals in fairy tales), people who are put under a spell by a witch or by hostile projections, turn back into beautiful princes or princesses, who are lovable and desirable, who can be happy and make other people happy.

If I wish the Angel of Love for myself or for you, I am not only wishing that you may be loved or that you fall in love with a man or a woman. Love is more than being in love. For me love is a quality of the self. In my cell I have an icon of St Nicholas. When I look at it, I feel that this saint is all love. Love simply shines out of him. He is not in love with a woman. Probably he is not in love with Jesus Christ either, but he is so imbued with love that he reflects it back with his whole being. This is a fundamental human longing, not only to love another man or woman but actually to become love. When you become love you love everything around you. You greet every human being with love and draw love out of them. You treat every blade of grass with respect and love. You know that, as the Talmud says, God has given every blade of grass an angel, to make it grow. You look at the setting sun with love. You feel you are loved by God, so that God's love streams through you. Everything you do is marked by this love. You do your work for love. If you sing, you sing because you love, because your love seeks expression.

People have always connected love with angels. To anyone who loves me I say: You are an angel. If I experience love, I have the feeling that an angel has come into my life. We need angels of love, to lead us into love's mystery, to put us in touch with the spring of love bubbling up in us, but which is often trapped or muddied by our sick emotions.

But you have to go carefully with the Angel of Love. You should not demand too much of it. It can only transform the material you offer it. If you repress and block your aggressive feelings, the Angel cannot penetrate them with its love. They remain in you like bitter coffee grounds. And gradually they will ruin all your efforts to love. Offer your Angel of Love everything that is in you, including your trouble and your anger, your jealousy and fear, your weariness and disappointment, because everything in you can be transformed by love. Let the Angel of Love accompany you in everything. Take it with you into your conflicts at work, your family quarrels, marriage, and friendships. The Angel of Love is not a sort of pious icing to spread over everything; it wants to transform your life. It forbids you nothing. It does not forbid you to feel annoyed. It does not demand you should not feel injured. It only wants you to allow it to shine through everything you experience. Then you will see your conflicts in another light. They will not just disappear. There will not always be quick and easy solutions. Your Angel of Love also loves truth. It wants you to look clearly at what has happened, to take seriously what you feel in any conflict. But it also wants you not to cling on to your injured feelings, but let them be tested by love.

First and foremost, loving does not mean having loving feelings. The word "love" is related to the Old Saxon word *liob* meaning "dear" or "precious." It requires belief, seeing that something or someone is precious or good, in order to love and be able to treat him or her well. So loving requires a new way of seeing. Ask your Angel of Love to give you new eyes, so that you can see the people around you and yourself in a new light, discover the precious core in yourself and others. Then you will be able to treat it more kindly. My wish for you is that your Angel of Love may lead you deeper and deeper into the mystery of divine love, which is like a spring in you that never fails. You do not have to create love in yourself. You have only to drink at the spring of divine love, which is bubbling up in you and is always enough.

2 The Angel of Reconciliation

First of all, the Angel of Reconciliation should enable you to become reconciled to yourself. Today many people are not at peace with themselves. They cannot reconcile themselves to the fact that their life has turned out differently from the way they planned it. They are at odds with their fate and the disappointments life has brought them. They are at war with themselves. They cannot accept themselves. They would like to be different, more intelligent, successful, and lovable. They would like to look better. They have a distinct image of themselves, which they would like to match up to.

The word "reconcile" comes via Old French from the Latin word meaning "bring back into friendly relations," just as the German word *Versöhnung* comes from Middle High German *süene*, meaning mediation, peace, kiss. There is a connection with "calming" and "making still." So reconciling yourself to yourself means to make peace with yourself, come to terms with yourself as you now are. Resolve the conflict between the different needs and wishes that drive me hither and thither. Heal the split there is in me between my ideal self-image and my reality. Calm my angry soul, which keeps resisting my reality. It means kissing what I find so difficult, my faults and weaknesses, treating myself tenderly, especially what in me contradicts my ideal self-image. For this I need the help of an angel, so that I succeed in becoming reconciled to myself, so that I can really say yes to my life story, my character, to all the baggage I have acquired on my way.

Only when I am reconciled with myself can I think about reconciling other people around me, who are at odds with me or with others. People who are divided and unreconciled with themselves will also cause division around them. Today there are many pious people, who conceal the split within themselves. Because they have too high a self-image, they split off the dark side of themselves. Then they have to project this onto others, so they continually see the devil or some demon in other people. They demonize those who do not live by the Church's rules, who do not correspond to their idea of Christian morality. Because they have split off the devil in their own heart, they see him everywhere around them. These people cause division around them. Some are enthusiastic because at last someone has come who is confident of telling the truth. Others feel that something sick and divisive emanates from this person, and they turn away.

The Apostle Paul understands Christian service precisely as a service of reconciliation. God has taken upon himself the service of reconciliation (cf. 2 Cor. 5:18). The Angel of Reconciliation wants to make you a messenger of reconciliation, not because you go about preaching and demanding that people around you become reconciled, but because you bring reconciliation. Reconciliation does not mean covering up all the conflicts around you with a cloak of piety, or that you have to iron out every difference of opinion and every disagreement. Many people confuse this with reconciliation. But really this is because they cannot cope with conflicts. They are afraid if everything is not harmonious around them. They are reminded of situations in their childhood that made them feel insecure, such as marital quarrels, which were threatening to them because they took away their feeling of safety at home. Reconciliation means peace-making. And peace-making means clearing the way for the different parties, building a bridge between quarrelling groups. But it does not mean smoothing everything over, making everything harmonious. Different points of view must remain. But they need not keep on fighting. There is a bridge by which the parties can again communicate, by which they can reach each other again.

Before you try to reconcile others to each other, before you can make peace in a quarrel between hostile groups, first you must become reconciled with yourself. And you must live at peace with the people around you. This does not mean that you must sacrifice all your feelings and needs for the sake of peace. On the contrary, if you suppress your annoyances for the sake of peace you will never become really reconciled with what has annoyed you. You must take your feelings seriously and you must not judge your feelings. They all have their meaning. If you get annoyed with a colleague at work, this is for a reason. Annoyance is the impulse to change something or see something differently. If I get annoyed when I am talking to someone and then piously suppress my annoyance, this poisons the atmosphere. If I express my annoyance appropriately, without judging it, this annoyance can clarify something. Annoyance often shows that the other person is not really being honest or forthright but is speaking in a roundabout way. If I express my annoyance, I give the other person the opportunity for self-criticism. I build a bridge between us, by means of which we can communicate better and more honestly. But it is crucial that I do not insist on being right. I must also respect the other person and try to become reconciled. Reconciliation means taking the other person seriously, but also taking myself and my feelings seriously.

Reconciliation has a political dimension. Unreconciled people not only divide the people around them. The division goes further. It helps form opinion in a country. It confirms prejudices against others who think differently or live differently. It creates an atmosphere of violence against foreigners and people who behave in a foreign way. So the Angel of Reconciliation wants to turn you into a leaven of reconciliation for our world. If you speak peacefully, reconciliation will come from you. Then foreigners and marginal groups around you will feel accepted. You will not sow split peas but seeds of hope and reconciliation.

3 The Angel of Exuberance

I find the word "exuberance" rather off-putting, maybe because I am a controlled rather than exuberant person. But perhaps, like me, you could do with a bit of exuberance. Being exuberant or unrestrained means letting go of my *persona*, the role I usually play, dropping the mask and giving outward expression to the liveliness within me. We call exuberant persons high-spirited. Their mood and their spirits are higher than normal. The word "mood" is related to the German word *Mut*, which comes from the Middle High German meaning strive, strain, habit, custom. So high-spirited people, whose mood is exuberant, do not live according to the normal habit of the daily grind, but with their own strenuous energy. Their heart is overflowing with the joy of life.

The Angel of Exuberance can give you the courage to trust your own liveliness. You must not always worry about what other people think of you, whether what you are doing conforms with the usual custom, meets other people's expectations. You just trust yourself and your own heart. Life wants to express itself. And life does not always flow along evenly. It can bubble over with high spirits, be childish and spontaneous. You can't just decide that now you will be spontaneous. That would be a contradiction. Either you are spontaneous or you are not. When you force yourself to be spontaneous then you have already ceased to be so.

Perhaps you are just disciplined. If so, you could ask the Angel of Exuberance to lead you to freedom. It requires distance from ourselves to allow ourselves simply to live as we feel. Too often we consider what other people will think, what impression we will make on others, if we behave in such and such a manner. Exuberance is freedom from worrying over other people's expectations. We set aside these expectations and trust to the life that is in us. We let go of the role we usually play. We drop the mask, which often enough contains our inner bounce.

Exuberance means sparkling liveliness. We cannot force it. Sometimes we feel lively. Everything pours out of us. Words just bubble up and out of us. Our mood is infectious, and everybody catches it. We have daft notions. This kind of exuberance often sparks off others. And it feels free. Other people also feel free for once to trust their own intuitions; the child in them that wants to play, without asking what for or what is the use. This child is in touch with itself. It lives for itself and not in accordance with the expectations of other people. When we are grown-up, we long simply to live like this again. We want to stop making life so complicated by all our worrying and weighing up what we can and should do and what other people want. My wish for you is that the Angel of Exuberance may lead you into this childlike freedom, so that you can enjoy life and freedom with all your senses.

4 The Angel of Safekeeping

"Safekeeping" means "awareness," "respect," "supervision," "care." It means that we are aware and careful about everything we experience, what we hear, see, and know. In our rushing lives we need the Angel of Safekeeping, not to keep us in the past, but so that we do not lose the treasure of our experience in the hectic pace of life. In our fast-living times we often lose sight of what we have seen. We flit from one impression to another. This means nothing can grow in us. We feel torn. We cannot properly taste what we have experienced. Today many people are incapable of living intensely in the present, of feeling what they experience. So they keep needing greater external stimuli to feel themselves at all.

The old monks developed a method of living completely in the present. This was the method of meditation, or as they also called it, *ruminatio*. To ruminate means to chew over. So they took the words from scripture into their mouth and kept chewing them over. They repeated them in their hearts, considered and reconsidered them, looked at the word from all sides. They could take a whole day over one word of scripture. The word became flesh in them. It changed them. It gave them something to hold onto in their spiritual unrest and the noisy world. It enabled them to live completely for the moment. Nothing was more important for them than to be present in the presence of God.

The Church Fathers had a neat saying, which compared the way we treat the word to the behaviour of the horse and the camel. The camel is content with little food, which it keeps chewing over. But the horse needs a lot to eat. It is never satisfied. St Anthony advises us not to be a like a horse but like a camel with the word of God. We should not keep stuffing ourselves greedily with more food but keep the little we have heard and read in our heart. Then it can change us. Then we can live off it. When he was in prison in Tegel, Dietrich Bonhoeffer wrote about how he called up memories and how they brought him light and comfort in the loneliness of his cell. He kept the memory of meetings, experiences at a church service or a concert in his heart and lived off them through that cold time. His ability to hold onto healing words and experiences gave an answer to Hölderlin's complaint: "Woe is me, where can I get flowers and sunshine, if it is winter?" Bonhoeffer kept the flowers of his experience of God, so that they could also bloom in the barren desert of a brutal Nazi dungeon. He kept sunshine in his heart, so that the warders' grim coldness could not threaten him.

The Angel of Safekeeping does not want to lead you into a conservative position, or a flight from the present. It wants to show you how to protect and treasure what is precious in your experience, so that you can always marvel at it. This gives your life depth and richness. It also enables you to cope with unpleasant situations. You can keep going through barren patches without dying of thirst. People who cannot store things up always need fresh comfort, fresh food, fresh experiences in order to feel they are alive. The ability to preserve things keeps me alive, even when I am cut off from life, in times of deadness or defeat. My wish for you is that the Angel of Safekeeping may enable you to live each moment intensely. May this Angel give you the power that Frederick had in the children's story, to gather the sunrays and the beauty of flowers into his heart in summer, so that he could live off them in winter.

5 The Angel of Leaving

Human beings have a deep longing to settle down in comfort, to make a home where they feel secure and protected. When we find somewhere pleasant we want to pitch our tent and stay there forever. But we also know that in this world we cannot ever set up a permanent home. We have to keep moving on. We have to keep departing. We have to leave the home we have built where we feel comfortable and go on our way. Leaving means leaving something behind. We have to leave behind our old life. We cannot just go on with it. I cannot always stay where I am now.

As long as we are on the road we have to keep packing up our tents, in order to reach the new country. At first every departure causes anxiety. We have to leave our old familiar life behind. And while I am leaving this behind, I do not know what is before me. The unknown makes me afraid. At the same time departure contains a promise, the promise of something new, somewhere I have never been or seen. If we do not keep moving on, our life will become paralyzed. If we do not keep changing, we will become old and stale. There are new possibilities for our life. But they can only take shape if we break away from old patterns

We want to settle down where we feel comfortable and at home. The disciples on Mount Tabor wanted to build three huts, so that they could remain forever with the blissful experience of the transfiguration. But Jesus did not let them. The very next moment the transfiguring light was obliterated by a dark cloud. They could not hang on to the experience, they had to leave and make their way down to the valley. There they would miss the mountain clarity. Every deep religious experience tempts us to settle down with it forever, to cling on to something we cannot hold. We cannot hold God. He is essentially the God of the exodus, the God of departure, the God who always tells us to leave. He speaks to Moses: "Why do you cry to me? Tell the people of Israel to depart" (Exod. 14:15). The people of Israel are afraid to leave. Of course they feel oppressed and enslaved in Egypt. But they have come to terms with the foreign government. At least their flesh pots are full. They want to leave, but at the same time they are afraid of departure. We frequently feel this same ambivalence. We are never content with our lives as they are. We are also afraid to leave, to leave behind the familiar life and risk an inner and outer change. But we will only experience life, if we are prepared to keep setting out on the road. For this, like the Israelites, we need an angel, who gives us the courage to depart, who holds his rod over the Red Sea of our fear, so that we can tread safely and confidently through our life's waters.

Today it is particularly difficult for the Angel of Leaving. The basic mood of our time is not to move on, as it was in the 1960s when there was a strong mood for change, created first by the Second Vatican Council in the Church and then in society by the student revolts. Today the mood is more one of resignation, self-pity, depression, gloom. We prefer to moan that everything is so difficult and we can't do much about it.

This is why we need the Angel of Leaving today, to give us hope for our time. This Angel will enable us to depart for new shores, give us the courage to create new ways of being together, a new way of behaving toward creation and a fresh political and economic imagination.

This also means that you must leave behind old preconceptions and outworn ideas. Removing internal blocks, opening up closed paths, giving up old customs and habits will enable you to set out for new ways of living and new stages of your life.

You will often hesitate because you do not know where the

way leads. Then may the Angel of Leaving stand beside you
and give you courage to go your own way.

6 The Angel of Community

We all live in some sort of community—the community of the family, the community of the Church, the community of our village or town. So what about the Angel of Community? The community in which we live is always threatened. It can break down if we do not communicate well with each other, if people just look out for themselves or dig in behind their own prejudices. The Angel of Community wants to help you to experience the gift of true community.

A glance at our own history is illuminating. For the first Christians, the experience that community was possible between Jews and Gentiles, men and women, rich and poor, was proof that the kingdom of God had come. In his own person and with the Spirit he gave us, Jesus Christ had joined people as different as his apostles together in a community. For the early Christians the community was the place where they experienced God. It can be so again for us today. A community of people praying in a religious service or prayer group can have an intense experience of God. We feel that we are not alone, that God is with us. Jesus himself promised us: "Where two or three are gathered together in my name, there am I in the midst of them." Or we are talking to a friend and suddenly feel an intensity, a sense that heaven is opening to us and our heart is expanding. When this deep stillness comes over us, it is no accident that we say, "An angel is passing over." The Angel of Community is creating a new quality of being together.

We also have the other experience, that the community can fall apart. Then we try to sort things out between us, but we do not succeed. We rub each other up the wrong way. When one conflict is settled, the next one breaks out. We feel powerless to pursue the ideal of community with which we began. We are disappointed, and we feel unable to grow together into a real living community. However, even this damaging experience can become a place where we find God. It can point you to the community of the angels where you are really at home, for there you can be yourself. There no one reproaches you. People do not project their own problems onto you. You need the Angel of Community to show you, in these dead-end situations, that there is still a deeper community, that you are involved in the community of angels. Then you feel that the ideal you have created of a Christian community cannot be fulfilled by your own efforts. In order to be able to live at all in this community, where there are so many conflicts and intrigues, so much human weakness and falsehood, you must have a deeper ground within you, a ground that is also beyond you. The community will never be able to fulfil your longing for home and security. It points you and your longing toward God.

A Hasidic story tells us that we can only live our own life if we are prepared to share it with other people. A Rabbi says, "Every human being is called to bring something to completion in the world. The world needs each person. But there are people who continually sit indoors studying and do not go out of the house to talk to others. That is why they are called unkind. For if they conversed with others, they would bring something of their allotted task to completion. So not being unkind to yourself means 'Do not spend too long by yourself without going out to others. Do not be unkind through loneliness.'" There is a good sort of solitude, which makes us fit for community. But there is also a bad kind of solitude, which isolates us. We shut ourselves up in it and so do not contribute what the human community expects of us. We do not make our own uniquely personal contribution to the community and thus in our own unique way make something of God's fullness appear in this world.

If you see the human community as a sign of the community God wants to give you, then you can enjoy it. Then you will always be grateful for the experience of being accepted. You know where you belong. There you can be yourself, just as you are. You do not have to prove yourself. You do not always have to fulfil expectations. You can let yourself slip. You can be weak for once. Precisely this is a sign of Christian community, that we can also show our weaknesses and our wounds. Henri Nouwen once said that everything that we withhold from the community will deprive it of liveliness. If we withhold our weaknesses, because we would prefer to hide them, then in an important way the community cannot flourish.

Community means sharing everything with one another, our strengths and our weaknesses. But there must always be room for our own secrets. There can only be community if each of us can also be ourselves. Because they want everything from their members, many Christian communities demand not only their money but all their thoughts and feelings. This oversteps the limit into the totalitarian. Community requires the breath and breadth of freedom. Solitude and community must be in healthy tension. If the community becomes absolute, we crowd each other so much we can hardly breathe. The community will only be fruitful when each of us in the community can also go our own particular personal inner way. It will require us to go further along the way. It will show us our blind spots, so that we go the way of truth. On this way of truth we arrive at new insights about ourselves and our fellows. May the Angel of Community keep on giving you the experience of being with others that is so demanding and brings such happiness.

7 The Angel of Calm

"To have nothing, to possess everything," describes the attitude of the wise in every religion in every age. Only those who do not set their heart on anything created, those who can let go of things others hang on to, are really free. Calm was an important word for the medieval mystics. In particular Meister Eckhart often speaks about calm. People are calm who have let go of their ego and given themselves up to God. They are those who have become peaceful at heart, because they have let themselves fall into the ground of the divine. For the mystics calm means liberation from our own ego, letting go of all cares and anxieties about ourselves, so that God can be born in our hearts, so that we can recognize our true self in our inmost being, our genuine personal core. This calm is an attitude of inner freedom, inner tranquillity, a sane distance from all the things that flood in on me from outside, threatening to "occupy" and possess me. This attitude is not easy. But it can be practised. In order to attain this calm I have to let go of many things.

First I must let go of the world. So say the mystics. St Anthony, the father of monasticism, left all his possessions in order to become free for life. We must stop hanging on to property, success, and recognition. If we hang on to earthly things we become dependent, and dependence goes against human dignity. Often enough we are dependent on our well-being, our habits, on people. A story told by the early Fathers explains by a parable how we can only enjoy through letting go: A child sees many nuts in a glass jug; he reaches into it and tries to get as many as possible out of it, but his clenched fist will not fit through the jug's narrow neck. First you have to let go of the nuts. Then you can take them out one by one and enjoy them.

Letting go is not an ascetic performance that we must force upon ourselves. Rather, it comes from a longing for inner freedom and the feeling that our life can only really be fruitful if we are free and independent. If we are no longer dependent on what others think and expect of us, if we are no longer dependent on the support and recognition of others, then we get into touch with our real self.

But calm detachment also means letting go of myself. I must not cling on to myself, my cares, my fears, my feelings of depression. Many people cling on to their injuries. They cannot let go of them. They use them to accuse people who have hurt them. In the end this is a refusal of life. We must also let go of our injuries and sicknesses. You need the Angel of Calm to teach you the art of letting go of yourself and your past, to show you how to distance yourself from yourself, stand back and look at your life from a different point of view, from a position beyond your own self. If you are calm in this way you can react calmly to the sensationalist reports in the media. You can reply calmly to criticism and rejection. Every criticism does not send you into a panic. You do not feel threatened. You are not afraid that the ground will be swept from under your feet. You have achieved some distance from all inner and outer disturbance. You know you are supported by the Angel of Calm, who tells you: "There is more than the opinion that others have of you. There is more than success and image. Let yourself go in God. There you will find firm ground on which to stand. From there you can look calmly at everything pouring in on you from outside."

If you are detached from yourself, you can react in a calm detached way to bad news. Reacting in a calm way does not mean receiving the news of a person's death with composure. Composure is the expression of an inner discipline. Even though composed people are shaken inside, they do not show their dismay. They restrain their behaviour and control themselves. Calmness does not mean self-control. Calm people do not need to restrain their behaviour, because they have a different point of view, because they are not inwardly hit by the bad news. Because they are detached from themselves and their idea of how their life should go, nothing can throw them off course that easily. The Angel of Calm helps them to regard everything they hear from the Angel's own distance. This gives them inner freedom and space.

Many people get carried away in a heated discussion. They say their conscience requires them to stand for the truth. The Angel of Calm shows you that in such a discussion truth does not lie in the rightness of the words or the arguments, but somewhere else, on a different level. Truth means harmony, agreement with reality. What we hold as absolutely true is often only the expression of our own projections. We make images of the truth for ourselves, images of God. Truth itself is incomprehensible. It cannot be defined. If we know about the deepest truth, we go calmly into the discussion, not resignedly, because we cannot know the truth. We know that our knowledge is always relative, that there can always be different points of view, that the truth will probably lie somewhere between the disputing parties.

Against the reasoning that insists it has the monopoly of rightness, the philosopher Martin Heidegger suggested a calm detachment and an openness to mystery: "You have to think constantly from the heart in order for both of these to flourish."

My wish for you is that the Angel of Calm may help you not to think too much with your head but also to listen with your heart.

8 The Angel of Passion

The Angel of Passion seems to contradict the Angel of Calm, but we need many angels to make our lives prosper. The Angel of Passion challenges us to live with all our heart, not just to exist on a low burner. If people are no longer capable of great passion, then their life is boring and insipid. They lose the taste for it. This is definitely not what Jesus meant; he told us to be salt for the earth, to season this world with our zest. Passions are natural driving forces in human beings, which drive them to live to the full and should drive them finally to God. The Angel of Passion should teach us the art of deploying these driving forces to make them forces for life. We should not be ruled by them but we can use them for our life's own purposes. We should not become driven people, who allow ourselves to be driven, but people whom passion drives to serve life and to create life in its many forms.

People who can get passionately involved in something can fight passionately for life. Their spirituality will also be passionate. A Hasidic story shows this: "A Hasid once complained to Rabbi Wolf about some people who spent all night playing cards. 'That's good,' said the Zaddik, 'like all people they want to serve God and do not know how. But now they are learning to keep awake and stick at a task. If they seek perfection, all they need to do is change the task—and then what great servants of God they will be!"

The old monks thought a great deal about the passions. Evagrius Ponticus (who died in 399) counts nine passions with which monks must struggle. For him the passions are positive forces. It is not a question of suppressing them, but of integrating them into your life. The passions should serve us, rather than us serving them. *Apatheia*, which is the goal of the struggle with the passions, does not mean a passionless condition but freedom from being pathologically ensnared by passion. It means integration of the passions in everything I do and think, a state in which the passions no longer rule me but are at my disposal as power, as *virtus*, as virtue, which helps make me alive.

Passions are value-free. Whether they are good or bad depends on how I act with them. Anger is a positive power, which can enable me to separate myself from something, free myself from the power of others. But it can also consume me, if I allow myself to be controlled by it. Sexuality can bring me to life, but it can also take me over. Fullness of living does not come from repressing or giving full rein to the passions, but from awareness in the way we handle them. Those who live without passion lack bite, lack force, lack fullness of life. Many Christians have killed off their passions by sheer striving for correctness. They have become boring. They are no longer the salt of the earth, no longer seasoning for our world, but insipid and dull. Jesus sided passionately with the poor and oppressed. He spoke passionately of the merciful Father, and fought passionately against the hardheartedness of the Pharisees, who had darkened God's image by their petty observances of the law.

The word "passion" comes from the Latin root *patiens*, meaning "suffer," just as *Leidenschaft*, the German word for "passion," comes from *leiden*, meaning "to suffer." This word *leiden* formerly meant to go, travel, journey. If you go somewhere you experience, you undergo something. Thus the word *leiden* gradually acquired the meaning of putting up with, bearing pain. So passion has to do with experience. If you suppress it, you lose experience. If you go with it, you experience the new, the unimagined. But just as every journey can be arduous, so can the experience of passion. It is always a balancing act. A passion can all too easily become stronger than is good for us. Then we do not live our own life with passion, but passion controls us. May the Angel of Passion accompany you in your balancing act, so that you can become a really passionate person, a person who engages passionately with others, and passionately fights to make it possible for us to live together on earth a life worthy of humanity.

9 The Angel of Truthfulness

We call people truthful when they are genuine and consistent. Jesus said of Nathanael: "Here comes a genuine Israelite, in whom there is no guile" (John 1:47). Truthful people do not live by calculation but by their own inner truth. They are free of intrigues, diplomacy, considerations of how best they can sell themselves to others. They live in harmony with themselves. They are genuine. They say what they think. They behave as they feel in their hearts. With such people you always know where you are. They do not hide their thoughts and feelings. They are not afraid to be known. They behave as they are, because they stand by everything that is in them. They hide nothing, because they have nothing to hide, because they are as they should be.

A truthful person is always free, for only truth can make us free. Today there are so many people who depart from their own truth. They are afraid to face the truth of their own hearts. They get into a panic when for once they have to be quiet. For then something they find unpleasant might well up in them. So they have to keep busy, simply in order to keep away from their own truth. They are always rushing and frantic. The worst thing that can happen to them is a moment when nothing is happening, when their own truth might come to light. If you evade your own truth you need a lot of energy to hide it from others. You are always wondering what other people are thinking about you. You rack your brain thinking about what you should say so that you sound all right to others, so that they do not start wondering about your psyche, your repressed drives, your complexes. You anxiously analyze every word in case it might suggest a neurotic complex or a repressed shadow.

The Greek word for truth is *aletheia*, which means things are not hidden. The veil is drawn back, and we see what actually, really is. Truthful people hide nothing; their true self is out in the open. The Angel of Truthfulness wants to keep opening your eyes to your true reality. The Angel takes away the veil that lies over everything. It removes the glasses with which you look at everything. Perhaps you are wearing dark glasses, which falsify everything. You only see the negative side. Or perhaps you are wearing rose-tinted spectacles. You are not willing to see people and their problems. You imagine things so that you can live more comfortably. The Angel of Truthfulness takes away all your glasses. The Angel shows you the reality. "When God sends his angel to the soul, it becomes truly knowing," writes Meister Eckhart.

A truthful person forces us to face the truth of our own heart. In the company of a truthful person we can hide nothing from ourselves. We find the courage to show our own truth. When Jesus spoke, then the unclean spirits, the troubled thoughts that plague people and harm them with poisonous feelings, could no longer hide. They were dragged out into the light by the word of Jesus. This is how Mark describes it. When Jesus preached for the first time in the synagogue, the unclean spirit in a man cried out. It felt that it could no longer hide behind critical and ironical expressions. It had to come out into the truth. What that meant was that the unclean spirit had to go out of the man, it had to set him free (cf. Mark 1:23ff). Jesus' truthfulness frees people from unclean spirits, which alter and falsify the truth. Jesus heals them, so that they become genuinely truthful people.

I wish you the Angel of Truthfulness, so that you can be wholly as you are in the depths of your being, so that you can free the people round you to the truth. Truth also means: the object and our knowledge of it coincide, the thing corresponds to our idea of it. They agree. My wish for you is that you may be wholly in agreement with yourself and the reality of your life.

10 The Angel of Gratitude

There is not much gratitude today. People make unlimited demands. They have the impression they will be sold short. So they need more and more. They have become insatiable and so are no longer capable of enjoyment. The French philosopher Pascal Bruckner describes people today as giant babies with limitless demands on society. They can never get enough, and it is always other people's fault when things go wrong. They are not given what they absolutely must have to live their life.

The Angel of Gratitude would like to bring a new taste into your life. It would like to teach you to look at everything with new eyes, grateful eyes. Then you can be thankful for the new day, that you have your health and can get up and see the sun rise. You are grateful for the breath that is in your body. You are grateful for nature's good gifts, which you can enjoy for breakfast. You are aware. Gratitude makes your heart open and joyful. You are not obsessed with the things that might annoy you. You do not begin the morning grumbling about the weather. You are not infuriated when the milk boils over. There are people who make their own lives difficult because they see only the negative side. And the more they see the negative side, the more their experience confirms it. Their pessimistic view of things attracts small misfortunes.

The word "thank" comes from "think." The Angel of Gratitude would like to teach you to think right and be aware. If you begin to think, you can thankfully recognize all that has been given to you in your life. You will be grateful not only for the positive roots you have in your parents, but also for the wounds and injuries you have received from them, because they have also made you what you now are. Without

these wounds you might have become self-satisfied and in-
sensitive. You would not see the needs of people around you.
The Angel of Gratitude would like to open your eyes to the
fact that an angel of God has accompanied you all through
your life, that a guardian angel has protected you from misfortunes, your guardian angel has transformed even your injuries into precious treasure.

The Angel of Gratitude gives you new eyes to become aware
of the beauty of creation and thankfully to enjoy the beauty
of meadows and woods, the beauty of mountains and valleys,
the beauty of the sea, rivers, and lakes. You will marvel at the
grace of a gazelle and the delicacy of a deer. You will no longer
walk unconsciously through creation, but thoughtfully and
thankfully. You will realize that a loving God touches you in
creation and wants to show you how extravagantly he cares
for you.

If you look thankfully at your life, you will accept what has
happened in it. You will stop rebelling against yourself and
your fate. You know that every day an angel comes into your
life anew, to protect you from harm and give you its loving
and healing company. Try to go through the coming week
with the Angel of Gratitude. You will find you see everything
in a new light, and your life will acquire a new taste.

You can also ask your Angel of Gratitude to teach you to be
grateful for the people you live with. We often pray for the
people who are important to us only if we want to change
them or if we want God to help them, heal, or comfort them.
Often our prayer for others is a prayer against them. We would
like them to become the way we want them. If we say thank
you for another person, then we accept them unconditionally as they are. We do not want them to change. They are
valuable, just as they are. People often notice if we are grateful for them. Our gratitude sends out a positive affirmation,
in which they feel themselves accepted as they are. An Ameri-
can clergyman tells the story of a married couple who had

prayed for many years for the wife's alcoholic father, that he would be able to get free of his alcohol. They offered their petition in countless prayer groups, but nothing happened. It was only when they gained the courage to say thank you for their father, that he was alive, that he was as he was, that they made it possible for him to change. Because he no longer felt unconsciously pressurized by them to change, he was able to change. Because he felt he was unconditionally accepted, he no longer needed alcohol. So ask your Angel of Gratitude for the miracle of making people feel unconditionally loved, because you are thankful for them, and for this love to keep them safe and sound.

11 The Angel of Renunciation

Things are difficult nowadays for the Angel of Renunciation. Many people associate the word renunciation with a strict asceticism. But God wants us to live life to the full. So why renounce things? Today life is all about consuming as much as possible, getting as much pleasure as possible. Of course there are plenty of examples of people who have become unendurable because they have given up so much. But must renunciation always lead to an attitude of enmity to life? Renunciation means giving up a claim to something that belongs to me. The goal of renunciation is inner freedom. If you have to have everything you see you are totally dependent. You are not free. You are determined from the outside.

Renunciation is an expression of inner freedom. If I can give up something I enjoy then I am inwardly free. Renunciation can also be a training in inner freedom. If, for example, I give up alcohol and meat for Lent, this can be a training in freedom. I test whether for six weeks I am able to give up television, alcohol, smoking, meat, perhaps even coffee. If I succeed I feel good. I have the feeling that I am no longer a slave to my habits, that I do not have to have alcohol to stimulate me. This gives me a feeling of inner freedom. It contributes to my self-respect. If I feel I just have to have coffee when I am tired, then I become dependent on it. Ultimately this annoys me. It takes away my dignity as a person with self-control. I feel I can no longer determine how I behave; I am dominated by my needs.

As a monk, I was once invited to take part in a television programme with a pleasure-researcher and a woman sex-researcher. The programme was called "Renunciation or Enjoyment or Both?" and we were asked about about enjoyment and renunciation. All three of us agreed that there can be no enjoyment without renunciation. If you want only to enjoy, you will not succeed. I can happily enjoy one or even two slices of cake. But by at least the fourth slice I am no longer enjoying it, just cramming it in. Today many people have become incapable of enjoyment, because they are no longer able to give things up. It used to be the other way round. Christians often made it difficult to enjoy life because they lived too ascetically. They were always suspicious of enjoyment. This was just as one-sided a view as the modern idea that we have to have everything. The greedy person becomes unable to enjoy. My wish for you is that the Angel of Renunciation may lead you to inner freedom. I hope it will make you able really to enjoy what you experience, really get involved in what you are doing, feel with all your senses what you are eating and what you are drinking. You will find that the Angel of Renunciation is also an angel of joy and enjoyment, who will do you good. If you give up your claim to what you are entitled to, food, drink, television, and the like, you gain yourself. You take your life into your own hands. The Angel of Renunciation would like to teach you the art of living your own life, freely disposing of yourself, so that your life is a pleasure to you.

12 The Angel of Risk

Today many people think the most important thing is not to be conspicuous, not to make a mistake. You must not leave your post. Then your career is not threatened. You will not be criticized in your group. Your life will be a success. In reality, this fear of taking risks is a hindrance to life. If you are determined not to make a single mistake you will do everything wrong. Because you dare nothing, risk nothing, nothing new can happen. In business and in politics, in both Church and society, no one is willing to take risks any more. For this would lay them open to attack, or things might go wrong, and that would be a catastrophe. They would no longer sit softly cushioned but have to stand up and face themselves and their mistakes. Many are afraid they would not survive this. They are so set upon the respect and recognition of others that they no longer trust their own instincts or risk anything.

Psychology tells us the fear of taking risks is connected with the lack of a father, so common in our society. Normally, the father is the one who gives us backbone, gives us courage to dare something or take a risk. If we do not have this positive experience of a father, our backbone will need support. So we lean upon an ideology or on what is regarded as normal. We play safe. We don't try any experiments. We do everything the same old way. We do not allow ourselves to think anything new, so we do not do anything different. There is no guarantee that the new thing will be successful. So we don't do it. Our life is marked by lack of imagination and lack of the courage to risk anything. The word risk comes from the Italian and means danger and daring. Many claim that life should go by without danger. You have to insure yourself against all dangers, so that nothing can happen to you. But the more you insure yourself, the more insecure you become. Gradually you no longer trust yourself. Everything has to be insured. We dare nothing without comprehensive security. This leads to greater and greater paralysis. We shall get out of the blind alley only if we take risks, if we dare to make mistakes.

My wish for you is that the Angel of Risk may give you courage to be daring in your life and to risk new ways for yourself and the people around you. May the Angel of Risk strengthen your backbone and keep your back free, so that you are free to risk yourself and trust your inmost impulses, without constantly needing insurance and support. The world will be grateful to you if you dare something new, if you do not first ask all and sundry for permission to put your ideas into practice. We experience every day that the old ideas will not do. No one dares follow a new course in the matter of unemployment. We prefer to entrench ourselves in commonplaces or pass the blame on to others. Everyone waits for someone else to take a false step. Then we can criticize them. But no one dares take the first step. We keep marching on the spot. We wait for others to make mistakes instead of risking a mistake ourselves. My wish for you is that the Angel of Risk should give you the strength and freedom to dare to make mistakes, to open up new ways for yourself and humanity. Only when you trust the Angel of Risk can you bring something new into the world, and then through you people can discover new possibilities.

13 The Angel of Confidence

Nowadays, when prophets of doom constantly alarm us with their visions of an apocalyptic future, we badly need the Angel of Confidence. Prophecies announcing the end of the world are booming at the moment. Of course no one can guarantee that our world will remain in balance for a long time to come and survive human follies. But the urge to prophesy the end of the world says more about the psyche of these self-styled prophets than about the reality of our world. Because they experience their own lives as a catastrophe and unconsciously nurture the wish that this ruined life should come to an end as soon as possible, they project their own situation onto the world and hope the world will end soon too. They express their inner destructiveness by describing the world's end in fire and brimstone. Because fear of the future is widespread today these false prophets often meet a willing response and so gain power over many anxious people.

The Angel of Confidence gives us hope and trust in the future. It enables us to see, to follow what is happening with our eyes, to see how God guides and leads everything, how God sends out his angel, so as not to abandon this world to evil but to turn everything to good. In this confidence I do not let myself be shaken by pessimistic forecasts. I do not put on rose-tinted spectacles in order to distort reality. I do not have any illusions about the state of the world. I recognize how it is. Nevertheless, I am confident. I know that this world is in the hands of God and his angels, that human beings have no ultimate power over it. This confidence sees more than what is immediately in sight. It sees more than the problems with which newspaper headlines bombard us. In addition to the external, it sees the inmost reality of things. As well as the world, it sees God's angels, who accompany us through it and keep their guiding hand over our country and our earth.

The Angel of Confidence was with the psalmist long ago. In Psalm 34:8 the psalmist prays: "The Angel of the Lord encamps around those who fear him, and delivers them." And in Psalm 91:11f: "For he will give his angels charge of you to guard you in all your ways. In their hands they will bear you up, lest you dash your foot against a stone."

Marie Luise Kaschnitz, the poet of the "Angels' Bridge," tells a story illustrating this confidence, about the ship owner Giovanni di Mata. He gave all his gold to the corsairs to buy freedom for their prisoners. As he was about to put out to sea with the freed prisoners, the robbers demanded more money. Because he could not meet their demands, they smashed his mast and helm and ripped his sails to shreds. Nevertheless, Giovanni di Mata gave the signal to set out. To the corsairs' astonishment, even without mast, sails, and helm, the ship slowly began to move and reached the open sea.

Likewise, the confident are given the knowledge that an angel protects us and shields us, that it even carries us in its hands, so that we can tread safely among lions and vipers. The confident believe an angel looks after them, so that nothing bad can harm them.

They do not walk blindly through the world. They see when danger looms. But they know they are accompanied by their angel. They know they are protected and supported. They know they are not just a number, at the mercy of fate, but that an angel goes with them, takes care of them, and frees them from all their fears.

14 The Angel of Solitude

Today many people are afraid of being alone. If they are alone they do not feel themselves. They need other people around them all the time just to feel alive. But solitude can also be a blessing. Without solitude there can be no real relationship with God and no genuine self-knowledge. Many people confuse solitude with being abandoned, with loneliness and isolation, but solitude is an essential part of every spiritual journey. All the great religious founders went through a time in the wilderness away from all other people. Jesus also endured solitude when he fasted for forty days in the wilderness. There he confronted his own reality and found God his Father in a new way.

So I wish the Angel of Solitude for you. I hope it will lead you into a fruitful loneliness, where you can get to know yourself as you really are, where you cannot make yourself interesting to others, but must confront your own nakedness. If you gather the courage to be alone, you can also discover how lovely it can be to be completely by yourself, not to have to show anything or prove anything, not to have to justify yourself. Then perhaps you may have the experience of being completely at one with yourself. The word "alone" says this, you are all-one. All-one in three ways. Firstly, you are wholly at-one with yourself. The longing for oneness was typical of the Greeks. They felt torn between different desires and needs. Today we understand this longing for oneness again. In our many-sided lives we too feel pulled about hither and thither by different offers and different struggles. Among the multiplicity I discover in myself, how can I find my own oneness, the clasp that holds everything together?

The second meaning of alone, all-one, refers to all humanity. It means being one with all, to feel a deep solidarity and union with all human beings. The more I face my own solitude, the deeper I feel my connection with other people. The old monks experienced this when they consciously chose solitude. They withdrew from people in order to become one with them at a deeper level. Evagrius Ponticus, one of the most important writers among the monks, expresses it thus: "A monk is a human being who has cut himself off from everything and therefore feels connected with everything. A monk knows he is one with all human beings, because he keeps finding himself in every human being." In my loneliness I discover my own depths, the ground of my being, and in these depths I am deeply connected with all human beings. There I feel that, as Ovid said, nothing human is alien to me, that in my inmost self I am connected with all other people.

The third meaning of being alone has to do with the All. Friedrich Nietzsche said: "Those who know ultimate solitude know ultimate things." In being alone I feel that I become one with all, with the ultimate, with the very source of all being. This experience of being alone is an essential part of being human. As Dostoyevsky rightly says: "Being alone from time to time is more necessary for a normal human being than eating and drinking." In solitude I feel what my humanity actually amounts to, that I have a part in everything, in the All of creation, and ultimately in the One who is all in all. If the Angel of Solitude leads you into this fundamental experience of your humanity, then you lose all fear of loneliness and being left alone. Then you feel that there where you are alone you are one with all. Then you experience your solitude not as loneliness but as homeliness, being at home. You can only be at home where the mystery dwells. Where the Angel of Solitude leads you into the ultimate mystery that rules our world, there you are never alone, there you are really at home. This mystery, which embraces all, gives you a home no one can take from you.

15 The Angel of Sisterhood

The Bible often speaks of *philadelphia*, brotherly or sisterly love. It was the happy experience of the early Christians that they were able to experience not only their physical siblings as brothers and sisters, but that the whole community became a community of brothers and sisters. May the Angel of Sisterhood and Brotherhood show you how many brothers and sisters you gain if you yourself approach them as a brother or sister.

The fundamental experience of the first Christians was that all the members of the Christian community had become their brothers and sisters. The reason for this was that they all had the same Father. Because we may all pray together to our Father in heaven, we are all brothers and sisters in his sight and under him. Jesus calls anyone who does God's will "brother and sister" (Mark 3:35). If we try to draw closer to this example, gather round Jesus Christ, and are prepared like him to do the Father's will, then we are Christ's brothers and sisters. Then a new family arises, in which we are all equal. Jesus forbids the disciples to call themselves Rabbi. "For you have one teacher, and you are all brothers" (Matt. 23:35). The Angel of Sisterhood can show us that we are all equal, that none of us should put ourselves above others. How often we place ourselves above others, not only through our social position, but especially through our prejudices. We feel we are better than others, we raise ourselves above them. We concentrate on their negative sides, and do not even notice how we project our own weaknesses onto others. There is a common mechanism by which we project our faults onto others, thus rating ourselves above them. We keep others away from us and so protect ourselves against having to look clearly at our own reality. Those who really know themselves stop trying to see their own faults in others. They become a real brother or sister to everyone, for they see themselves in everyone.

Having a sister is different from having a brother. I am lucky in my family because I have three sisters and three brothers. There is my eldest sister, who often took our mother's place when we were children. There is the Angel of Sisterhood, who looks after us like a mother. She is not the big mother who swallows us, but she gives sisterly loving care. She does not stand over us but sits beside us. She is tender and understanding. She discovers needs that a mother cannot fulfil. Then there are sisters of the same age, companions on the way. With brothers you go together through thick and thin. With sisters you have intense conversations and you touch strings in yourself which with brothers would remain mute. Then there are younger sisters. It is not for nothing that we often give them "angelic" names. The Angel of Sisterhood brings me into contact with my *anima*, my emotional nature and my spirituality. Angels have always stood in a sisterly relation to our souls. Helmut Hark, evangelical priest and therapist, speaks of the erotic relationship between our soul and the angel who is our spiritual companion. If we look at angels in an art book we often discover their erotic aura. They awaken passion in our soul, which otherwise only a lover stirs. Angels' erotic power has a healing effect on us.

The experience of a sister can bring us into touch with our inner angel. The sister herself can become an angel, who makes music with the tender strings of our soul, who brings the spiritual energies in us to life and heals our broken heart. So I wish you may meet many Angels of Sisterhood, and I wish that you yourself may become a stimulating Angel of Sisterhood who brings others to life.

16 The Angel of Self-Surrender

Maybe, at first, self-surrender sounds very passive and re-signed. People who do not succeed in actively shaping and controlling their life simply surrender themselves to fate. They give up on themselves. However, this is not the way the Angel of Self-Surrender would want to lead us. It means something quite different. First of all, self-surrender has something to do with letting oneself in for something. Those who surrender to life let themselves in for life and its activity. They do not hold themselves back. They do not clench up within themselves but surrender to the flow of life. Something can come alive and blossom in them.

Self-surrender is the opposite of keeping a firm hold on yourself. Many people cling fast to their own image, others cling to their habits or possessions, their profession, their success. The Angel of Self-Surrender would like to lead you into the art of letting yourself go, surrendering yourself to life, ultimately to God. I can surrender myself only if I trust that I am not surrendering to an arbitrary fate but to an angel, who means well by me. Those who surrender to their angel become free of unnecessary cares, which plague people today. Their life stops revolving around themselves and their health, recognition, and success. This attitude of self-surrender consists not only of trust but of great inner freedom. When I do not have to do everything myself, when I simply surrender myself to God, trusting that he will take care of me, I become free of all self-absorption and self-centredness.

The Angel of Self-Surrender would also like to help you trust enough to surrender yourself to another person. Many friendships and marriages today fail because the partners hang on to themselves, because they are afraid of self-surrender. They

fear to lose their freedom, that the other person will domi-
nate them, that they will become victims of his or her whims
or even ill will. But no relationship can succeed without this
self-surrender. It is bound to fail if the partners anxiously take
care to control their emotions, words, and actions, so as not
to give themselves over to the other. Then no trust can grow,
the other person cannot show that he or she means well by
you and will not abuse your trust. Self-surrender does not
mean giving up on yourself. I can only surrender myself if I
am in touch with myself, if I know who am. But at the same
time there is always a risk in this self-surrender. I lose the security of holding onto myself and surrender myself to the other
person. This can succeed only if I know that the other means
me well, is not a devil but an angel who will catch hold of me
and carry me safely.

I know many people who think they have to do everything
by themselves. They work hard by themselves in order to get
on and realize their ideals. They struggle to do good. But at
some time or another they reach the point when they realize
that they cannot get what they want. They have so many good
intentions, but they cannot fulfil them all. Again and again
they are confronted with their own inadequate reality. This is
the time to open up and surrender to the angel God has sent
to make your life succeed. This is not resignation but freedom. I realize I do not have to achieve everything I wanted
to; that was simply my own ambition and by no means the
will of God. When I stand before God in meditation and hold
out my empty hands to him, I feel the freedom that comes
from self-surrender. I let myself rely on God. I know that God
supports me, that in God's kind hands I can be simply as I
am. This is the core of belief in Christ: the experience of the
freedom with which Christ has made us free (cf. Gal. 5:1).

17 The Angel of Warmth

It is often said of people that they give out warmth. You feel good when you are with them. Other people emit cold. When you are near them you freeze up even in summer. The Angel of Warmth would like to make you able to give out warmth, so that people near you feel secure and loved. It would like you constantly to be able to find people who become an Angel of Warmth for you, so that when you are with them you can thaw out your frozen feelings, you can warm yourself in their company, if this cold world has made you feel cold. Many people today find the world cold. This means that you cannot often take off your protective overcoat when you are with others. People are afraid to be at the mercy of others' cold gaze. We all barricade ourselves behind a wall of cold. So Angels of Warmth could do us good. They make meeting and intimacy possible. They create an atmosphere in which we feel good, we feel at home.

The question is what can you do so that the the Angel of Warmth makes you able to give out warmth to the people round you. For me it is important that I keep warming myself in the warmth of God's love, so that I have a warm heart for others. Henri Nouven sees the spiritual life as tending an inner fire, which burns in all of us. Nouven thinks many people today are burnt out, because they have opened the door of their stove too wide to the outside world, so they cannot keep up their glowing heat. It will quickly turn to burnt-out ashes. For me too spiritual life means tending the inner fire. It helps me when I am meditating to fold my arms and imagine I am now closing the door of my stove, so that now the fire of God's love can glow through everything in me and transform it. Then I feel a pleasant warmth inside me, and I know

that the fire of God's love extends to all. I do not have to resolve to show warmth to everyone. If I tend my inner fire
through prayer, I become warm inside, and this warmth will
be enough for all the people I meet today.

You cannot fake a warm glow. You cannot plan it in ad-
vance. When I look at the Gothic paintings of angels, especially Fra Angelico's angels, they warm my heart. They are
angels from whom warmth radiates. In them there is nothing
gloomy, nothing cold, nothing hostile. What Paracelsus once
said about angels is true of them: "You should know: An angel is a human without the mortal part." Because angels lack
what is mortal, destructive, and pathological in humans, the
warmth that goes out of them warms us without burning. If
I look at these angels I feel how this warmth does me good.
Then I will find that warmth also goes out from me. I should
be grateful for it. The warmth that goes out from me, which
can warm others, does not deprive me of my own warmth. It
warms us all because it is fed by the source of divine warmth,
because it constantly blazes up with the fire of divine love.

The Angel of Warmth will make you able quickly to warm
to others and others to you. Warmth will radiate back and
forth. This will not make you grow cold. On the contrary,
the warmth that radiates back and forth will grow warmer. It
creates an atmosphere that other people also can enjoy. If I
am in a group I can feel at once if there is a cold atmosphere,
if people have to be careful of every word they say. Or I can
feel if there is a warm atmosphere, an atmosphere of good
will and friendliness. Then each word does not have to be
weighed. There I can be as I am. There I am accepted completely. My wish for you is that you should always feel the
Angel of Warmth around you and that you yourself may become an Angel of Warmth for others, someone who gives out
warmth, which warms other people's hearts.

18 The Angel of Courage

The German word for courage is *Mut*, which is related to the English word "mood." The original Old High German word *muot* meant "to strive for something, violently long for something, yearn." It corresponds to the Greek word *thymos*, which denotes the disposition, the emotional side of the soul. From the sixteenth century onward, the German word *Mut* has increasingly acquired the meaning of bravery. Bravery is one of the four cardinal virtues. It means being unafraid in the face of danger. According to the ethicist Demmer, it arises from good sprits and demands willingness to make sacrifices, the power to carry things through and the will to assert yourself. Courage and bravery are required not only of soldiers but of everyone. We all need courage to live our own life, the life to which we were destined from the start. All too easily we adapt to others, take on their ideas, and do not swim against the current. Today a liberalism prevails that permits everything. But at the same time we observe a great uniformity. The media establish norms, of how we should behave nowadays, how we should think, how we should dress, what we should do. It requires great courage to be different, to be what is right and fitting for myself.

You need the Angel of Courage if your fellow-workers are demolishing a colleague. It requires courage not to join in the carping, if you say maybe it would be better to speak to her instead, or if you break off the conversation with the remark that all this could be seen in another light. You may be misunderstood. Perhaps the others will accuse you of being a Pharisee. The woman is quite impossible. People won't be put off so easily. If you have the courage to interrupt gossip about someone else, the scandalmongers feel caught out and may want to justify themselves by turning on you. Then you need strong courage to assert your opinion, even when the others try to exclude you and accuse you of being very ready to gossip about other people yourself.

May the Angel of Courage stand at your side when you have to make decisions, decisions about your career or life choices. Marriage, a life-long commitment to another person, is just one of these choices. People accuse their contemporaries of being weak about taking decisions, of putting them off and preferring not to commit themselves. Every decision binds me, at least for the time being, and I am very much afraid of this commitment. For important decisions you can ask the Angel of Courage to help you. You can never have a guarantee that your decision is absolutely right. There is never an absolutely right way for us. Nevertheless, when we come to a crossroads we have to decide which way to go. We have to choose one way or another if we want to go on. Every way sometimes leads to a narrow pass, through which we must travel for our lives to go on. Jesus tells us to go through the narrow gate along the narrow road (cf. Matt. 7:13f). The broad road is the road travelled by all. You have to find your own personal way. It is not enough to take your direction from others. You must listen carefully to discover your own way. Then you must bravely decide to go this way, even when you feel very lonely on that road. Only your own personal way will enable you to grow and really live your life.

Life keeps presenting you with tasks you have to deal with at once, otherwise it will be too late. Life punishes those who come too late, said Gorbachev, and this saying has become famous.

The Angel of Courage can help you to do what is required immediately. This could be a conversation to sort things out in your family or at work. It could be facing a problem that everyone else at work has put off. It could be a visit you have long postponed and are still avoiding. It could be a letter you

finally have to write to clarify a relationship or sort out a mis-
understanding. There are so many situations in your everyday life when you need the Angel of Courage, so that you do
what has to be done and do it now.

19 The Angel of Patience

Waiting patiently is out of fashion nowadays.

> Blessed are those who wait.
> The globe whistles past them.
> The sharpest bit of the world
> doesn't deter their gaze
> from the promised direction.

So writes the poet Ulla Hahn. The Angel of Patience illustrates something of this beatitude, that the Kingdom of Heaven belongs to the patient.

The word patience comes via French from the Latin word *patiens*, meaning suffering. *Geduld*, the German word for patience, comes from the Old High German *dulten*, to bear, endure; it is connected to the Latin *tolerare*, meaning to tolerate. In the New Testament the Greek word used for patience, *hypomene*, actually means "to be under" or "stay under," to endure, to hold out. Sometimes patience is regarded too passively, as if it were a matter simply of accepting things as they are. In the early Church, the meaning of patience was closer to endurance, steadfastness through the hardships threatening Christians from the outside world. In his Letter to the Romans (5:3) Paul says: "Suffering produces endurance, endurance produces character and character produces hope." And his Letter to the Colossians (1:11) prays: "May you be strengthened with all power, according to his glorious might, for all endurance and patience with joy." Here *hypomene* means "steadfast endurance, as needed in battle when a man must defend the position in which he finds himself against all enemy attacks." This is definitely relevant to our lives today. It means steadfastness and the power to hold out against all external attacks. Here patience is not passive suffering but active endurance and holding out. It is "enduring resistance." Paul relates it also to forbearance, *makrothymia*. For him this is a fruit of the Spirit (cf. Gal. 5:22). The Greek word means that you have great courage, great character, a big heart, making you able to wait. In the course of history the word patience has taken on both meanings: steadfastness, endurance, and also the ability to wait, forbearance, watching patiently until a solution is found.

May the Angel of Patience make you able to wait. This is not an obvious quality today. We always want a solution at once, but often it takes a long time for a flower to bloom. We need patience for our own development. We cannot change ourselves all at once. Transformation happens slowly and sometimes unnoticeably. The Bible images still speak to us today. Jesus gave us the parable of the seed that grows by itself (cf. Mark 4:26-9). James also takes farmers as an example in his letter: "Behold the farmer waits for the precious fruit of the earth, being patient over it until it receives the early and the late rain. You also be patient" (James. 5:7f). Many people want instant success as soon as they have begun something. In therapy they want instant progress, and in spiritual counselling they want instant results. This determination to control their success leads them to overlook what is slowly ripening in them. They urgently need the Angel of Patience, to give their inner processes time to develop. Growth requires time. Everything that shoots up fast also withers fast.

Patience does not mean refusing to consider everything that can be changed and should be changed. But we should also be patient with ourselves and with any situation that cannot be changed and demands calmness. May the Angel of Patience also stand by us, if we have to bear something, if we have to endure a painful situation. Marriage problems or conflicts at work cannot always be solved quickly or at all. There too we need patient endurance in a painful situation, one that cannot quickly be changed, in which we can only hope a solution will be found. But patience does not mean coming to terms with the conflict permanently or an uneasy compromise. Patience includes the power to work toward change and transformation. Time also plays an important part in patience. We give ourselves and other people time for something to change.

We need patience when we are ill. We cannot get over it all at once. Today the power simply to endure something is becoming rarer. Patiently to hold out, to endure, to keep going, is a virtue that is not often asked for today. Nevertheless, we need it urgently in order to cope with our life and to confront the problems of our world with hope. Therefore I wish you the Angel of Patience, so that you do not give up at once if you are in a difficult situation, if a problem seems insoluble. May the Angel of Patience give you the power to carry something through and the confidence that change will happen.

20 The Angel of Lightness

Pope John XXIII once wrote in his journal: "Giovanni, don't take yourself so seriously!" He treated himself with something of the easy lightness that the Angel of Lightness could teach you. Perhaps the Italians find it easier to deal with this Angel than the heavy Germans, who take everything so seriously, with thoroughness and rigour. There is a time for everything. Of course it is right really to tackle difficult problems. For this you need the Angel of Courage. But especially with personal problems, this thorough approach is not always the answer. The more directly we attack our faults, the more strongly they resist us, and then we develop a running battle with them. Then we could do with Pope John XXIII's light touch. This was a pope who took his office more lightly than many of his predecessors who collapsed under the burden of it. But it was Pope John XXIII who had the courage to call a Council, which set the course for the future.

Above all, we need lightness in our dealings with ourself. Many people cannot make any progress because they take themselves so very seriously. They cannot forgive themselves if they still have faults that people of their age should no longer have. So they make a concerted effort to stamp out these faults. But the more fiercely they attack their faults, the stronger they grow. Finally, these earnest battlers lose patience with themselves. Either they become even stricter with themselves or they give up the struggle. The Angel of Lightness would like to teach us another way. We are not satisfied with our faults, but we combat them with humour. We do not take things so tragically if we fail once again. We take our human weakness lightly, because we do not have to take it all upon ourselves, because we know that we are in God's hands. Those who think they have to solve everything feel a heavy responsibility; for them being human is a very hard task. Lightness does not mean light-headedness or negligence. It is based on a deep trust that we are in God's good hands and that he takes care of us. We know that we do not have to prove anything to him. That is why it is not so bad if we fail sometimes, because we cannot sadden him by our failure. We only upset ourself when we do not come up to our own expectations.

The Angel of Lightness would like to lead us into a new freedom in our dealings with others. Anyone who, like me, lives in a monastic community knows that you should not take everything so seriously. Otherwise life becomes artificially difficult. In the monastery we are and remain human beings. Of course that is true not only of a monastery. Every mother bringing up children knows that there is no point in constantly getting upset about their faults. Here too lightness is needed, because she trusts that her children will get over their childish naughtiness and grow up one day. They are only children. They are allowed to make mistakes. They need to learn from their own mistakes.

Children who experience this lightness in their parents will have more confidence in life than other children whose parents take everything very seriously, parents who think bringing up children is like doing a PhD, which they have to pass. Those who try to bring up their children perfectly usually achieve the opposite.

Lightness also comes from the confidence that the children are not just my children, their development does not depend only on my "perfect" upbringing, but they are also in God's hands. God sends his angel to care for every child.

If we look at the angels rejoicing over the Christmas crib, or the *putti* of baroque paintings in countless churches, we feel something of the lightness that radiates from them. They do not take life as seriously as we do. They hover and fly over many things that we cling on to, that we are determined to sort out at all costs. The artists understood something of the angels' lightness, which is offered to us to lighten the heaviness of our life and give us lightness of being.

21   The Angel of Openness

There are many people you cannot meet because they are locked inside themselves. They have built defences around themselves, so that no one can get through. They have hidden themselves behind a mask, because they are afraid someone might discover their true face. They do not want to reveal themselves, because they are afraid of truly meeting anyone. They are afraid of their own reality. The Angel of Openness wants to open you up to the mystery of meeting. You can only meet other people if you are open to them, if you open your heart and let them in. For me, the archetype of such an open meeting is the meeting between Mary and Elizabeth, which we read about in Luke chapter 1. Mary sets out. She leaves her house, the place where she is protected, and goes over the hills. She goes over the mountains of prejudice, which often prevent us truly from meeting someone, and over the hills of inhibitions, which keep us from going out of ourselves. She goes into Elizabeth's house and greets her. She doesn't just greet her cousin out of doors but goes inside her house, into her heart. They are both open to each other. Thus the mystery of meeting can take place, which transforms them both. Then both come into contact with the original image of themselves that God made for them. The child in Elizabeth's womb jumps for joy that she remembers the true image of God in herself. In Mary she recognizes the mother of her Lord. In her *Magnificat* song of praise Mary recognizes her life's mystery. She knows the Lord has regarded the lowliness of his handmaid and done great things to her. If we meet each other as openly as Mary and Elizabeth, this meeting will transform us too, and open our eyes to the mystery of our life.

May the Angel of Openness open you to the future, for what

God has in store for you. Many have settled themselves so firmly in their life that they are no longer open to anything new that God brings them. Everything has to remain as it was. People like this are often fossilized. You should be open to the new possibilities God offers you. New things can only develop in you if you are open to them, if you do not cling to the old, if you do not freeze onto your life as it is. This openness shows itself in a readiness to take on new ideas, to learn new ways of behaving, to meet new challenges at work, in your family, and in society. Open people are prepared to keep learning new things in their profession, to get stuck into new technology and developments. Open people remain awake and lively.

Openness with other people also means uprightness and honesty. If you speak your opinion openly to others, they know where they are. People who are so open are a blessing to us. They will not speak about us behind our backs. We can also be open with them. Their uprightness does us good. Even if they tell us unpleasant things, we know they mean us well. They do not hide their preconceptions and prejudices behind a façade. They show themselves as they are. They confidently tell us the truth because they feel free. They are not dependent on our agreement. Because they are at peace with themselves, with their uprightness they can also accept rejection by those who cannot bear their criticism. May the Angel of Openness give you such uprightness and honesty, so that with inner freedom you can tell other people what you feel in your heart. Of course such uprightness also requires good sense and sensitivity. You must feel what you can say to the other person and when you would just hurt unnecessarily. But because you are not set on being popular at all costs, you are free to tell the truth. Look at the Angel Gabriel and the way he tells Mary about the birth of her Son. The artists made the Angel a figure of openness for the woman he visits. He tells her something new and unimagined. With his openness he opens Mary to the apparently impossible. May the Angel of Openness open you up to the mystery of human meeting and to the new things you are capable of.

22 The Angel of Sobriety

Sometimes we use the word sober to mean unimaginative and boring. But this is definitely not where the Angel of Sobriety should lead you. Originally the German word *nüchtern*, meaning "sober," is a monastic word. It comes from *nocturnus*, meaning "nightly." The monastic nightly office or vigil has three nocturns or night watches. It took place before breakfast. So *nüchtern* means "not having yet eaten or drunk anything." If you have not yet eaten, you are wide awake, you are aware of things as they really are. If we have drunk a lot, our mind may be foggy and have only a faint grasp of reality. When we have eaten a lot, we are full up, sleepy, and incapable of taking in very much. So sobriety means seeing things as they are, without looking at them through sleepy eyes or projections.

Such sobriety is needed in a discussion when people are ruled by their emotions. This sobriety is a blessing, if clearsightedness in a decision is threatened by too much self-interest, too much of a power struggle, or too many conflicts in the relationship. A craftsman told me about the problems with decisions he encountered in a convent. One of the nuns said she wanted a yellow curtain, not because she liked it but because the mother superior wanted it, and the other nuns, who could not stand her, were determined to have a green curtain. Quite often our decisions are affected by such conflicts in relationships. Then we need the Angel of Sobriety to enable us to see clearly what is right. Sobriety also means objectivity and truth to the facts. If we are true to the facts, we will also be true to him who is the ground of that reality.

But often we mix up the facts with our emotions, so we can no longer see them correctly. Then we can no longer solve a conflict, because everyone is floundering in a morass of emotions, which they cannot get out of on their own.

The Angel of Sobriety could be a blessing to you when you are talking to people who are seeking your advice, telling you their problems, their injuries, their troubles and disappointments. If you do not enter into the quagmire of emotions with them but soberly clarify what it is all about, then you can really help, you can help advice-seekers find a way out of the morass of their emotions. Sobriety requires a proper distance from others. If you are awash with sympathy you cannot show other people the way. Perhaps your sympathy does them good at first. But it is not enough for you just to have a good moan together about how awful life is. You should sympathize with others. But you also need to take a sober look from a fair distance, in order to find a way out of the jungle.

The Angel of Sobriety can also help you to assess your own situation correctly. It can help you stop exaggerating and dramatizing yourself and find a way to sort yourself out. Often you are blinkered and see things only in terms of your annoyance, disappointment, or hurt. This prevents you from seeing practicable solutions. I wish you the Angel of Sobriety, so that you can see your own situation clearly, and can bring clarity into the fog of human conflicts about relationships and decisions.

23 The Angel of Forgiveness

Forgiveness and and pardon may sound like being soft. Other people may take advantage of me, and as a Christian there is nothing I can do about it except forgive them. I am not allowed to defend myself. I must even forgive my worst enemy. The Angel of Forgiveness does not want to humiliate you and leave you defenceless, but wants to free you from the power of people who have injured and hurt you.

You should not suppress your own feelings when you forgive someone. Forgiveness always comes at the end of anger, not at the beginning. In order to be able to forgive you must admit the pain the other person has caused you. But you should not wallow in it, otherwise you will do yourself harm. As well as being conscious of your pain you also need to be angry about it. Allow yourself to feel angry about what has hurt you. Anger is the power to distance yourself from what has hurt you. Anger enables you to throw the person who has hurt and upset you out of yourself. Only when you have thrown him out can you then consider: "He is only human, a hurt child too." Or you can pray like Jesus on the cross: "Father, forgive them, for they know not what they do" (Luke 23:34). Perhaps you think other people know exactly what they are doing if they hurt you, if they play upon your guilt feelings, or mercilessly touch your most sensitive spot with their criticism. Yes, they know what they are doing. But perhaps they do not know what they are really doing to you. Perhaps they are so enmeshed in their own concerns, their own fear, their own despair, that they cannot do anything else. Perhaps they have to make you look small, because this is the only way they can believe in their own greatness. Perhaps they are full of inferiority complexes, so they have to make another person look smaller than they feel themselves. If you think like this, the other person has no more power over you. Only when through your anger you have freed yourself from the other person's power can you really forgive. Then you feel that this forgiveness does you good, that this forgiveness finally frees you from the power of the person who has hurt you.

Often it takes a long while before we can really forgive. We should not disregard our feelings. If your father keeps hurting you, first you need the anger to enable you to distance yourself from him. Perhaps this anger must grow even stronger so that you are no longer affected by his authoritarian strictures and constantly putting you down. As long as the knife that has wounded you is still stuck into you, you cannot forgive. You would only injure yourself even more. You would push it further into the wound. That would be masochism. First you have to throw the other person out of yourself. Then you can really forgive. Otherwise forgiveness would merely mean giving yourself up, acquiescing in your own unhappiness. Many people never get over what has hurt them, because they have never forgiven. Forgiveness frees you from the hurts that people have caused you, it heals your wounds.

Once, when I was running a course, I invited the participants to imagine three people who had hurt them, to feel the pain and anger, and then to forgive them. Then I realized how many people are going around bearing old wounds, which keep boring deeper inside them. They need the Angel of Forgiveness, so that their wounds heal and they become free of people who still have a hold over them. Unforgiven injuries cripple me. They use up the energy I need for life. Many never heal because they remain unforgiven. But the Angel of Forgiveness gives you time. It never demands too much.

Human beings cannot live together without forgiveness, because whether we want to or not, we will keep hurting one another. If we keep counting the injuries we have done one another, this can become a vicious circle. If we disregard them, they will generate bitterness and aggression in us, which we will blurt out at any opportunity in the form of reproaches, criticism, resentment. At some time, we will bring them home to others and this will create guilt feelings in them. The Angel of Forgiveness breaks the vicious circle of recrimination. It clears the air and makes it possible for us who are constantly hurt and constantly hurting other people nevertheless to live together as human beings.

24 The Angel of Freedom

We all long for freedom, because we find it painful to feel dependent. If other people control us, if when we are with them we can do nothing but fulfil their expectations, this makes us angry. It is against our dignity. Or, if we are controlled by our emotions or our habits, we do not feel happy. Of course, today we have political freedom. But many people feel unfree in their dealings with others. They feel bound by certain constraints. They are ruled by the expectations of society. They do not trust themselves to break out and swim against the current. They feel that others determine how they are. No one has the confidence to say freely what they think. They consider what others expect of them, what others will think about them. They are not themselves but try to be as others would like them to be. But if this is the case I can never become a human being, I can never discover who I am.

The English word "freedom" and the German word *Freiheit* come from the Indo-European root *prai*, meaning protect, look after, care for, love. The ancient Germanic peoples called anyone they loved and therefore protected "free." These people were entitled to belong freely in the community. They were free, independent, unhindered, and unrestricted. I feel free if I know I am loved. Then I do not have to adapt myself to other people's expectations. I can be as I am. If I feel loved by people, when I am with them I can behave as I feel. I do not always have to be afraid what the other person will think of me. I know I am accepted. If I know I am loved in the depths of my being, I am free from the pressure to fill other people's expectations. I am free from the pressure of always having to be successful, always having to prove something, having to meet society's standards.

The Greeks had three words for freedom: *Eleutheria* is the freedom to go where I like. I am free to act. I can do what I feel is right for me. I am not constrained by the rules and expectations of others. *Parrhesia* means freedom of speech. Perhaps you think that is nothing special. In a democracy you can say what you think. But think how often you take your line from others. I know a very gifted person, who has good references. But he cannot find work, because at every interview he keeps worrying about what the head of personnel will think of what he says and whether he would be considered neurotic if he were to use this word or that. He is not free in his speech. We are only free if we can show ourselves as we are, when we can express our truth to others. The third Greek word, *autarkia*, means self-rule, self-determination. I can decide for myself what I want, what I eat and how much, when I fast or go without. This inner feeling of freedom, of being my own master, is an essential part of human dignity. Today many people are driven by their cravings. Here the Angel of Freedom could do you good and allow you freely to determine what you do.

A woman has fallen in love with a man. But he is not interested. Although she knows the relationship has no chance, that she will only get hurt, she cannot break away. She could do with the Angel of Freedom to give back her dignity, the feeling that she is valuable, that she does not need to run after this man. Other people feel constrained and unfree in their marriage, their family or community. They have no room to breathe. They also need the Angel of Freedom to give them inner freedom. Inner freedom means that no one can have power over my inner self. This inner freedom gives me independence even in friendship. I do not define myself in other people's terms. I am always myself. Such freedom is necessary for friendship or marriage to succeed. If two people cling to one another, if they always have to check what the other person is thinking, this restriction makes it impossible for a mature relationship to grow. Wherever I am tied, I also need my freedom. I bind myself in freedom. I leave myself a space which no one else can dispose of. My wish for you is that the Angel of Freedom will give you that inner freedom to feel you really are a free person and can live as one.

25 The Angel of Parting

Parting is painful. Saying goodbye to someone you love can break your heart. But you have to. We cannot hold on to others. They want to go their own way and have to in order for their life to succeed. We have countless partings in our life. We have to say goodbye to familiar surroundings, because we want to study in a different place or because we have found work somewhere else. Only when we have said goodbye properly can we really get involved in the new experience and let something new grow in us. Many try their best to cling on to all the people they have become close to. They want to keep a friendship going for always. But there are friendships that are good only for a time. Then they just drag on. They are kept up through a sense of duty or so as not to hurt the other person. But they no longer work. This would be the right time to say goodbye. This is only fair to others. I am confident that they can go in another direction. Then I am free to begin something new.

One kind of parting is particularly painful. That is parting from a husband, wife, or partner with whom you had planned to spend your life. Today many people suffer this painful parting. A relationship breaks up. A marriage cannot go on, because you are only doing each other harm and making life hell for each other. Instead of a clean parting, many fight their divorce in court and remain at war. Love turns to hate. Relationship therapists have developed parting rituals, to say goodbye properly. It is appropriate in such a parting ritual that I put into words all the good experiences I have had with the other person, that I thank the other person for everything he or she has given me. Only then can I say why, despite all this, we must part. So we can both go our own way, without having to write off the years of our life we have spent together. I can gratefully accept them and then go forward in freedom, without bitterness, reproaches, or self-laceration.

But we don't have to say goodbye only to people. We have to say goodbye to habits, life-phases and life-patterns. If you have never said goodbye to your childhood, you will always keep nurturing infantile wishes. If you have never said goodbye to your puberty, you will always be a prey to the fantasies about life you dreamed of then. We have to say goodbye to our youth if we want to grow up, to our bachelorhood if we want to get married, to our job when we retire. But above all we must say goodbye to the injuries we have suffered during the course of our life. Many people cannot live a good life because they still hang on to the hurt they suffered in childhood. They still blame their parents for bringing them up so narrowly, for not meeting their needs. In order to live my life here and now with full awareness, I must say goodbye to the injuries I suffered in childhood. Here and now I am responsible for my own life. Never mind what my childhood was like, now I can make something of what I got from it. No one's experiences were all good or all terrible. As well as hurt, we also received healthy roots from our parents. But we can only discover them if we have consciously parted from our parents.

May the Angel of Parting help you to say goodbye to old life-patterns, with which you make your life difficult—for example, the pattern of perfectionism, which compels you to control everything, or the pattern of self-injury, which drives you always to blame yourself or put yourself down. You must let go of the pattern of always having to perform well to prove your worth to your mother. Perhaps now your mother's place has been taken over by school or church, and you wear yourself out for them. But you are still following the same old pattern. If we do not say goodbye to old life patterns, they impel us to hurt either ourselves or others, or unconsciously to seek situations in which we continue to be hurt as we were in child-hood. Perhaps you look for a boss who puts you down in ex-actly the same way as your father did. Perhaps you find a girl-friend who is as possessive as your mother was. May the An-gel of Parting help you to say goodbye to your past and your old life patterns, so that you can live completely in the present, realize your potential, and let new unimagined things grow in you.

26 The Angel of Mourning

When we mention mourning we immediately think of mourning for someone who has died. This is the most solemn mourning. If you do not mourn a dead person you have loved, your mother or father, for example, you will block the flow of your life. You don't know why you can't really enjoy yourself, what the something is inside you that prevents you living your life. It is often because you have not mourned. In mourning we consciously concentrate on the loss of this person whose death has so affected us. We look again at our relationship with him or her. We remember everything we experienced with him or her, what the person meant to us, what he or she gave us. But we do not disregard the difficulties we had with this person, the pain we suffered, the things that we never expressed or made clear. Many people are astonished that there can also be anger in mourning. But so there should be. Mourning clarifies our relationship and sets it on a new level. If we have gone through mourning, we can build a new relationship with the dead person, the dead person becomes a companion. She has not simply disappeared. We often meet her in dreams. She may even say things to us that help us. Or she may simply remind us that we needed something that she provided. By going through mourning we discover who the other person really was. During her lifetime we knew only one part of her. The other part was hidden behind a mask. Now we know what she actually wanted to say in her life, what the deepest longing of her heart was, what message she wanted her life to give.

But the Angel of Mourning does not want to teach you only how to mourn properly for the dead. There are many occasions on which it could teach you the art of looking back at

the past and leaving it behind you. There is mourning for all
the life you have not lived. I meet many people who have the
feeling that life has tricked them. They have never been able
to live the life they would have liked. Their parents and teachers pushed them in a direction that was wrong for them. Or
they painfully recognize what their childhood was really like,
how they never really experienced security. Such knowledge
is very painful.

Mourning is necessary. Otherwise these things continue to
determine us and creep secretly into all our thinking and doing. Then we do not realize why we react so over-sensitively
in certain situations or perhaps freeze up. That is because we
have not mourned the disappointments life has brought us.

However, we do not suffer disappointments only in childhood. Throughout life we experience relationships breaking
up, our lives being smashed. We fail. All the ideals we wanted
to fulfil have proved to be illusions. Now we are disappointed,
disillusioned, listless. A man once told me that after the break-
up of a relationship he felt as if his wings had been cut off.
The Angel of Mourning wants to protect you from going
through life with clipped wings. It would like to give you new
wings, so that you can fly into the air and look down from
above on your failures. It would like to give you new impetus
to take on the tasks that are now before you. However, the
Angel of Mourning cannot protect you from the pain that
comes with all mourning. You must lay yourself open to this
pain. You can be sure that you are not alone with your pain;
the Angel of Mourning is with you and will transform your
pain into new life. Perhaps the Angel of Mourning will also
send you people who can be with you in your sadness, who
understand you, who can feel with you and open your eyes
to what new possibilities are now before you.

27 The Angel of Transformation

Angels come in different shapes. They possess the art of transformation. They may change themselves into a human being to accompany us on the way. They transform themselves into a doctor who heals our wounds, a therapist who shakes us out of a neurotic pattern, a priest who releases us from our sense of guilt. "Angels come unexpectedly," says a modern song. Sometimes it is your friend who says something to you that makes you see everything in a new light. Sometimes it is a child who looks at you and shows you how unimportant the problems you are racking your brain with are.

Angels are quick-change artists. The Angel of Transformation wants to lead you into the mystery of your own transformation. If you want to stay alive you have to keep changing. If you do not change you become fossilized. C. G. Jung once said that the greatest enemy of change was a successful life, because successful persons think everything is fine. They need never change. So such people stand still, both outside and inside. They repeat the same ways of talking they have been using for the last twenty years. They resort to the same solutions, which have always worked. They become boring. There is little pleasure in conversing with them. The way they speak and think has grown stale, or is like cold coffee that no longer tastes good.

The Angel of Transformation wants to prevent you from being too hard on yourself. Many people think they need to change themselves. But changing is often hard and involves self-rejection. I must change, because I am no good the way I am. I must finally overcome my faults, my over-sensitivity, my fear, my bad temper. This resolution to change contains the idea that all my faults and weaknesses are bad. The Angel of Transformation would like to tell you that everything in you is good, that everything in you is allowed to be there. Everything that is in you has its meaning. But it also needs transforming. Fear is good. It often shows you that your life is based on a false premise. Perhaps you think you should do everything perfectly, you should not make any mistakes. Then your fear shows you that this way of thinking is damaging you. It invites you to adopt a more human approach to your life. Your anger is good. If you listen to it, if you get to the bottom of it, your anger can become transformed into a new life energy. Perhaps your anger is showing you that up till now you have always geared yourself toward others. Now you can finally live for yourself. So your anger can change into new energy.

Fairy tales know about the mystery of transformation. Human beings become animals and animals change into human beings. This shows you that you should not be frightened of anything that is in you. Everything can be transformed in you too. There is a beautiful fairy tale that describes the mystery of transformation. It is the tale of the three languages. In it a young man does not learn what his father wants. He learns the language of barking dogs, the language of frogs, and the the language of birds. When in his wanderings he comes to a castle, the lord of the castle offers him only the tower in which wild barking dogs, who have already gobbled up many others, are kennelled. The young man is not frightened because he understands the language of dogs. The dogs tell him that they are only so wild and fierce because they are guarding a treasure. They show him the treasure and help him to dig it up. Then they disappear, and peace comes to the land. I like this story. Where your chief problem lies, the thing that makes you suffer the most, where you are sick, is also where your treasure lies. That is where you can come into contact with your true self. The story tells you that everything in you has a meaning. If you are constantly discontented and angry, this does not mean you should reject yourself. You should ask yourself what treasure these feelings are pointing you toward. When you have dug up your treasure, when you have found your true self, you will be at peace with yourself. You are grateful that the barking dog attracted your attention to the hidden treasure. May the Angel of Transformation give you the courage to treat everything in yourself gently, because everything in you is material for transformation, until finally your true self shines through.

28 The Angel of Enthusiasm

I always find people who can be enthusiastic about something refreshing. They have an exciting idea, perhaps about how they could rearrange their work, and they are enthusiastic about it. Or they are on holiday and are full of enthusiasm about the wonderful landscape. They are enthusiastic about an evening when they were together with friends and had a good time. They are enthusiastic about new paths. They can sweep others along with their enthusiasm. They experience everything intensely. They point out how wonderfully the sun is shining through the clouds, how extraordinarily beautiful the mountain is towering over the valley.

On the other hand there are people who no longer feel enthusiastic about anything. They go on holiday just the same. But when people ask them how it went, they immediately start complaining about how they did not like the food or how unsatisfactory the hotel was. They constantly need fresh impressions from outside in order even to feel themselves. But the further they travel and the more money they spend on their holidays, the less they experience, the less alive they feel. They seek life outside themselves because they have no life inside. But they do not let what they experience on the outside into themselves, so they never live really intensely.

People who can be enthusiastic are moved by a word, a look, a meeting, the forest through which they are walking, a mountain they climb. They are excited by looking at a wonderful landscape. They are shaken out of their remoteness. They come out of themselves and get wholly into what they are experiencing. The Greeks spoke of "ecstasy," meaning to be out of yourself, and "enthusiasm," meaning to be in God. So ultimately enthusiasm could mean letting myself be drawn into God, who accompanies me in everything, in creation, in humanity, in every word, in music, in art. Only in God do I experience the whole mystery of a human being, of nature and art. In God I experience their depths. What I ultimately touch in everything is God.

People who can be enthusiastic can sweep others along with them. They radiate life. They don't just sit around in the evening and moan about things. They sparkle with enthusiasm. They have ideas and want to make us enthusiastic about them. They can tell us enthusiastically about their experiences. They are lively and fresh. Conversation is not desultory. It is always exciting. There are always new ideas and new plans. It awakens our pleasure in life. We suddenly feel like going to this concert, visiting that exhibition, going on that ramble. Such people enliven us and fill us with spirit.

My wish for you is that the Angel of Enthusiasm will enable you to be enthusiastic, to be moved by the things you encounter, what you experience, and what you are. I wish you may also make other people enthusiastic, so that you can sweep them along with an idea, a project, enliven them and fill them with spirit. Then the Angel of Enthusiasm will give you joy in life and transform you into an Angel of Enthusiasm for the people you meet.

29 The Angel of Healing

When we hear the word healing we immediately think of healing our sicknesses, our own health. The word health is related to the German *heil*, which originally meant to be "well, hale, saved, whole, complete, fresh, unweakened." As a noun it meant "happiness, health, healing, help, salvation." The Angel of Healing would like to give you hope that your life will succeed, that it may become whole, that you can accept everything that is in you, say yes to everything you are, that you can say, "It is good as it is."

In order for you to be able to say this, you must first heal your wounds. Each of us bears wounds. We were hurt by our parents, even if they meant well. We were hurt if we were not taken seriously in our uniqueness, if our needs and feelings were simply ignored, if our fundamental needs for love, security, safety, and dependability were not fulfilled. We were hurt by teachers who made us look foolish in front of the class, by priests who filled us with the fear of hell. We were hurt by a boyfriend or girlfriend if we quarrelled, if they touched us in a sensitive place, if they put the knife into our wounds. Wounds can heal and will heal. Of course healing does not mean that you simply do not feel them any more. But they will not constantly fester. A scar grows over them. Then they will be part of you, without stopping you from getting on with your life. They will no longer use up all your energy. They will even keep you sensitive, they will become a source of life for you. Through the Angel of Healing your wounds will become a precious treasure, a precious pearl, as Hildegard of Bingen says. Where you were wounded, there you will be open for the people around you, you will react sensitively if they tell you about their own wounds. There you yourself will be alive. There you come into contact with yourself, with your true self. May the Angel of Healing give you hope that all your wounds can heal, that you will not simply be defined by the history of your injuries, but can live wholly in the present, because your wounds no longer stop you getting on with your life. On the contrary, they enable you to live. The Angel of Healing would like to transform your wounds into a source of life and blessing for yourself and others.

When the Angel of Healing has healed your wounds, you yourself will become an Angel of Healing for others. Then other people will feel well when they are with you. They will feel that they can show you their wounds, that you understand, that you do not judge their wounds but simply accept them. They will feel that you create a healing atmosphere. You do not project your wounds onto them. You do not just talk to others about your problems but are also ready to listen to them. They can tell you about their injuries, without being afraid that you will brand them as sick or as mere moaners. You really will not know why people like to come to you and why they speak to you so openly. It is clearly the Angel of Healing who has transformed your wounds and now wants to communicate to others in you and through you: you are good as you are. You are whole, healthy, and your wounds can heal.

30 The Angel of Faithfulness

Today faithfulness is no longer expected. Too many people have seen how a bride and groom swore to be faithful at their wedding. Then before long the marriage breaks down. Many people are afraid to promise to be faithful to another person, because they know very well that they cannot give any guarantee about themselves and how they may feel. Nevertheless, we long for people who are faithful, who stand by us and make us feel safe and secure. Longing for faithfulness in others corresponds with our doubts about whether we ourselves can be faithful.

The English word "true" originally meant "steadfast, strong as a tree." As we often do not feel as steadfast as a tree, which has deep roots and cannot be easily toppled, we also fear that we cannot be faithful to each other, that we cannot give any guarantee about ourself. Faithful does not simply mean being faithful or true to your principles or your task. That should be called fulfillment of duty. Faithfulness is always faithfulness to someone, faithfulness to a person. Faithfulness requires love. I can only be faithful to someone I love. Faithfulness contains the longing that I can entrust everything to the person I love, that I am constantly ready to answer the call of the person I have bound myself to. Faithfulness is not something static, but the readiness to go on a journey with someone, and the promise to be faithful and reliable through all my own wanderings. Through all life's changes and chances, I only reach my own self by committing myself faithfully for the future. As the German philosopher Otto F. Bollnow says, human beings become themselves only through faithfulness, by which they find their own permanent self in life's constant ebb and flow.

If we promise to be faithful to another person we can never guarantee ourselves. Neither should we. When I took my vows in my religious Order, I made a promise to my monastic community. But I have no guarantee that one day I will not fall so deeply in love that I can no longer live in that community. But I am helped by God's saying that he is faithful. The Second Letter to Timothy has words I find very comforting: "If we are faithless, he remains faithful, for he cannot deny himself" (2 Tim. 2:13). The fact that God remains faithful to me, even if I am unfaithful, gives me the certainty that my life will succeed, whether or not there are internal or external breaks in it. That takes away my fear of binding myself to be faithful to my community.

If we say someone is faithful, we do not just mean marriage partners who are faithful to one another and do not stray. We also mean people we can rely on. We do not have to keep courting their favour. They are faithful to us, and that does us good. Even if we have not heard from them for a long time, we know we can count on them. With another person we have known for decades that he will write to us at least once as year. This is not a burden to him. We are clearly so important to him that he faithfully keeps up this contact with us or wants to meet us. When my sister was in Italy as a young woman, she met a married Italian sociology professor. They each went their own way, and their lives underwent many inward and outward changes. But thirty years later they are still in friendly contact. If she goes to Italy she can always visit him. If he is abroad he gives her the key to his flat. This is a faithfulness that does us good, because we can always count on it.

My wish for you is that the Angel of Faithfulness may be at your side and that people come to you upon whom you can rely. May the Angel of Faithfulness make you able to be faithful. Then you will experience how you do good to other people and how you find your true self amid all your heart's changing fancies. Faithfulness should not be expressed in spectacular oaths of loyalty. It is shown in your reliability, in your readiness to stand by others all through their life, go with them through all their changes, without turning away. A blessing lies upon such faithfulness. In such faithfulness we feel the angel, who empowers us, because we cannot do it on our own. By such faithfulness people feel supported and carried through all the inconstancy of our world. They know that they are important to someone. That helps them to see their own worth and to stand by themselves in spite of all their disappointments.

31 *The Angel of Tenderness*

People who love each other sometimes tell each other: "You are an angel of tenderness to me." Thus they express how much good it does them that the other person is so tender to them, that they do not feel treated like a possession, but like a precious treasure, which should only be handled with care. However, tenderness is not just the way two people treat each other when they are in love. Today it has become a modern virtue. In the midst of a world dominated by violence, young people yearn for a different way of relating to each other, an atmosphere of tenderness. They create their own culture of tenderness, their own lifestyle of tenderness. Tenderness is the art of treating other people, nature, and all things tenderly. Although the idea of tenderness is modern, we find the phenomenon of tenderness in all ages. The Bible is full of tender encounters. The Letter to Titus tells us that in Jesus Christ God's tenderness (*charis*, meaning grace or tenderness) has appeared (Tit. 3:4). Before his death the writer Heinrich Böll demanded a theology of tenderness. He himself found in the New Testament a theology of tenderness "that always heals."

May the Angel of Tenderness introduce you to the art of treating people tenderly and delicately, and not only people but everything you deal with. The word tender goes with loving, beloved, valuable, close, delicate, beautiful, soft. You can treat others tenderly only if you are fond of them. Then you will not put pressure on them, you will not criticize or treat them brutally. You will not force them to give up all their secrets. You approach them with care and tenderness. You can speak tenderly to them and behave gently. In such a tender atmosphere, in which others feel respected and precious, in which they discover their own beauty, tenderness expresses itself in tender gestures, in a tender touch, stroking or kissing. In such tenderness love flows between people, a love that does not cling, that makes no claim to possession, a love that lets go, that respects, that has a feeling for the other person's mystery.

Behaving tenderly toward things means that when I pick up a book I hold it carefully in my hands, because it is precious to me. I am often shocked by the brutal way in which many people treat books. When they have read a book they throw it aside. Brutality, the psychologists tell us, is often an expression of repressed sexuality. Tenderness is the expression of an integrated sexuality. Sexuality flows into everything I do in life, everything I touch, all the work I do, all my dealings with people and things. I treat the cup and saucer tenderly when I put them on the table. Tenderly I pick up the tool I am going to work with. St Benedict wanted the steward of a monastery to treat all equipment like altar vessels. Ultimately in everything we touch we touch the Creator.

I wish you may find Angels of Tenderness, who treat you tenderly, who create a tender atmosphere for you where you can flourish, you can be wholly yourself, you can let go of yourself, and you feel all right. I also wish that you too may be an Angel of Tenderness for others. In order to be so, you must first go to school with the Angel of Tenderness, so that you deal tenderly with everything you meet and touch. Thus you will create a tender space around yourself in which others feel secure.

32 The Angel of Cheerfulness

For the early monks *hilaritas*, cheerfulness and inner clarity, merriment and brightness were the sign of a harmonious spirituality. If you know the truth about yourself, if you have experienced your own heights and depths, if you feel wholly accepted, this *hilaritas* shines out of you. You no longer walk through the world with a gloomy face. Nothing human is alien to you. You know that everything is in safe hands, even your own weaknesses and the errors of humanity. You shine from within, because inside you everything is lit by the healing, warming light of God's love. The root meaning of *heiter*, the German word for cheerful, is clear, bright, cloudless, shining. A bright light shines from cheerful people upon their surroundings. It drives away the clouds that darken human minds.

Cheerfulness is not just a disposition you are born with. It arises from deep trust that we are unconditionally accepted as we are, that ultimately everything is good. It arises from the courage to look at our own truth. Christians are convinced that only those who let God's light penetrate into the depths of their souls can shine with cheerfulness. There are no dark places in them they must hide, no abysses to terrify them. They walk carefree through the world. This is not naive optimism but an attitude that comes from meeting the truth. Because they have come face to face with their own truth, they no longer need to trouble their head over possible problems and dangers. They are not obsessed with the dark side of this world; they see everything bathed in divine light. They are confident that this light, which has conquered their hearts, will also prevail in the world.

This cheerfulness is infectious. When you are with a cheerful person you cannot converse about the end of the world. You cannot indulge in moaning about how terrible things are in the world. Cheerful people do not shut their eyes to the real situation of this world. They do not repress the dark side of things. But they see everything from a different perspective, ultimately, the perspective of the spirit, which also looks through the darkness until it finds God's light. They see everything from the angel's perspective, who sees this world's reality as it is, but who manages to rise above it on wings and, despite all the difficulties, regard it with inner cheerfulness.

You cannot frighten cheerful people. They are at peace with themselves. So nothing can easily upset them. If you talk to such people, you begin to feel cheerful inside yourself, you see yourself and your life with new eyes. It does you good to be with these cheerful people. You know how depressing people can be who look at everything gloomily, who are obsessed with the negative, which they discover everywhere. A cheerful person cheers you up. You suddenly feel lighter. I wish you may meet many Angels of Cheerfulness. Likewise, I wish the Angel of Cheerfulness may make you feel brighter inside so that you become cheerful and light, shining and cloudless, and the world around you also becomes bright and cheerful.

33 The Angel of Devotion

Children devote themselves to a game with total dedication. Nothing disturbs them. In the game they forget themselves. They give themselves up to the game. The artists of the baroque period often represented angels as children, playing with complete dedication. The Christmas angel painted by Matthias Grünewald on the Isenheim altar is completely lost in its violin playing. The art historian Wilhelm Fraenger says that for Grünewald angels are "vessels of heavenly joy and rapture . . . the quintessence of self-outpouring bliss." So angels in art are the soul of dedication. They are completely in the moment, they devote themselves wholly to what they are doing just then. It was said of a Jewish Rabbi after his death that the most important thing for him was the thing he was doing at the moment. Clearly he had been initiated by the Angel of Devotion into the art of giving himself up completely to the moment.

Researchers may devote themselves to their work. They do not let go until they have found the solution. Artisans can ply their craft with devotion. Ultimately, devotion has to do especially with two areas of life: devotion to love, in sexuality, and mystical devotion to God. Devotion in love shows most clearly what devotion means in my life. The sexual act is the climax of devotion. The partners forget themselves and give themselves up completely to the other, into the other. They fuse into each other. They abandon themselves, letting themselves go completely. They do not cling on to their fear that they might lose themselves. They can lose themselves because they know they are falling into loving arms.

What sexuality experiences at its climax happens in every love. If you love another person you dedicate yourself to him

or her. You no longer want to stay by yourself. You want to
be with the other person. You want to devote yourself to the
other person, because he or she means everything to you. This
devotion makes it possible to experience a new richness. If
you abandon yourself to the person you love, your love will
make you feel richer and more alive and freer than before.
Many people cannot abandon themselves. They are full of
mistrust that their devotion may be abused, that they may
lose themselves. People who try to control everything, who
control their feelings, their partnership, their words and actions for fear of making a mistake and showing their weakness, are incapable of self-abandonment. They lack an essential part of successful living. Those who cannot abandon themselves will ultimately always remain alone. They cannot really
meet other people. Without self-abandonment we cannot love
and we cannot live.

It is said of the saints that they abandoned themselves wholly
to God. They put themselves at his disposal. They prayed that
God would do as he liked with them. It is difficult for us to
pray such a prayer of utter self-abandonment. But through it
the saints became free. They could go forward full of trust in
the future. They knew that whatever God planned for them
would ultimately be good. The prayer of St Nicholas of Flue,
who died in 1487, is famous: "O my God, my Lord, take me
away from myself and give me wholly to you." This prayer
turned him into a mystic, made him become completely transparent to the reality beyond our reality. Thus he could be a
peacemaker for his contemporaries, an angel who showed
them a new way, because he kept himself out of conflicts and
saw everything from God's perspective.

This devotion does not mean giving up on yourself but finding yourself in a new way in God. Jesus says that this self-
abandonment is necessary in order for our lives to be fruitful.
Pious folk often use all their religious activity as a way of hanging on to themselves, to their security, their salvation. Then

their lives are unfruitful. They will never experience the richness and life that comes from self-abandonment.

May the Angel of Devotion teach you the art of dedicating yourself to your work, to the people you love and to him who is Love itself. Devotion will richly reward you. It will lead you to freedom and to a fathomless trust that your life will be good. You can let go of yourself. You feel you are carried. The armour you have acquired by clinging on to yourself will fall apart. You will feel you are alive and can expand. Your life will become fruitful. By devoting yourself you flourish.

34 The Angel of Harmony

Psychology dislikes the word "harmonize." People who can't stand conflict or bear any difference of opinion want to sweep all disagreements under the carpet and harmonize. They set up an artificial harmony that makes any progress impossible. The problems go on festering and will break out again. People who harmonize in this way are afraid of the truth. They cannot stand quarrels. Perhaps they feel so negative about quarrels because they experienced their parents quarrelling so often in their childhood. When their parents quarrelled, they were frightened they would be left alone and lose their parents' protection. So every quarrel makes them afraid that the floor will drop from under their feet. So they harmonize, trying to pretend that there is really no quarrel, that everyone is right. An even worse way of harmonizing is constantly moralizing that we must bear with each other, because as Christians we should love everybody.

The Angel of Harmony does not want to teach you to harmonize, but to show you the art of living harmoniously with yourself, how you can live in agreement and in tune with yourself. The Greek word *harmozein* means to fit together. You will attain an inner harmony if you fit together all the contraries that are in you. You are aware of the contraries in yourself. You let them be. So they no longer tear you apart. You arrange them with each other. You let each part of yourself have its own sound, so that everything is in concord. Thus you create harmony in yourself. You are in tune with everything that is in you. You do not have to repress anything in yourself or exclude anything from the harmony. Everything that is in you must make its own sound. Whenever you suppress parts of yourself, your rage or your fear, they will be missing from your soul's music. Then there can be no real harmony.

If you are in tune with yourself, you can create harmony around you. But this is not an artificial harmony, created by harmonizing. It is a bringing together of all the different opinions and disagreements and all the people with different points of view. Nothing is swept under the carpet. The different viewpoints are looked at and formulated clearly. Every opinion is respected and not immediately judged. All are allowed their point of view. This is openly discussed with others. Problems are talked through until everything is sorted out, until all can accept a solution with which they can live, which does not destroy their own coherence. This is not artificial harmonizing but finding a way in which people can go forward together despite their differences.

Harmonious people will also create a working atmosphere around them in which people enjoy working. Every discord is followed by harmony again. People who are in tune with themselves do not need intrigues to whip people up against each other. They create an atmosphere of clarity and harmony around them. Everyone feels respected. Everyone can join in the one great symphony of the company or the community. So my wish for you is that the Angel of Harmony will make you become an Angel of Harmony for others, so that they can find the courage to sound their own quite personal note.

35 *The Angel of Clarity*

Many people can formulate quite clearly what a discussion is all about. They listen to the arguments. They feel the emotions that play their part in the conversation. They identify quite clearly what the actual problem is and what the solution should be. Or in a personal conversation they tell you quite clearly what you have overlooked until now, where you are blocked and what you need to change, so that things will go better for you. This is not something they have learnt. They are not professional psychologists, but they have clear insight into what is going on. They do not say a lot, but when they do speak they hit the nail on the head. They clear up something that was murky and opaque. They are an Angel of Clarity for you. They are like Filippo Lippi's angels, whose faces reflect a bright transparent clarity.

The Angel of Clarity would also like to come to you and draw out the qualities you already have within you. Probably you have already had the experience of seeing everything very plainly, that all at once everything was clear. For the ancients, this was the mystery of enlightenment, this suddenly seeing everything clearly. I do not see anything in particular. But all at once everything is clear to me. I can say yes to my life. I feel that everything is good. I do not see anything concrete, but I see into the depths, where everything becomes clear. Experiences like this are always a gift. Everything becomes clear; we see through the shadows to what actually is. We come into contact with true being and with the original and undistorted image of our own self.

You will also be familiar with the experience of suddenly becoming clear about what you should do, what your personal vocation is, what way you should go. You have clearly seen how things are around you. All at once you understand yourself. Maybe you have been worrying about yourself for a long time and could not make any progress. But suddenly, as if from heaven, came a flash of light, which made you see yourself clearly. That was when the Angel of Clarity visited you and opened your eyes to reality. Or you had to make a decision. For a long time you were unsure what you should decide. There were so many reasons for and against. There were so many possibilities between which you could choose, a profession perhaps. All at once you became quite clear about what you should go for. Then the Angel quite obviously touched you, and brought clarity to your divided heart. Or you had got into a messy situation. You had not seen clearly what was going on. But suddenly everything became clear to you. Once again you felt the presence of the Angel.

The Angel of Clarity would like to help you know yourself clearly, to see into your own depths. Once you become expert at this, you can become an Angel of Clarity for others. Then in a conversation you can also suddenly see clearly what others actually need, what would do them good. You can bring clarity into their muddled thoughts. They will be grateful to you. You cannot just learn this clarity. You need the Angel of Clarity to initiate you into it. You can pray that the Angel of Clarity will come to help you if a friend in a difficult situation asks to talk to you. Then you will not go into the conversation feeling you are under pressure to perform, as if you absolutely had to help or solve your friend's problem. You can have a relaxed conversation, because you trust that the Angel of Clarity will come to your aid and enable you to clarify and be of help. Perhaps you will not be able to say anything for a long while, because you do not understand anything. All at once you will feel a slight impulse. You say something and it is right to the point. Then you know that the Angel of Clarity has come to your aid.

36 The Angel of Slowness

"The Devil invented haste," says a Turkish proverb. We speak of "heavenly peace." The Angel of Slowness can remind us of this paradisal quality. The novel *The Discovery of Slowness* has become a cult book. Obviously the author, Sten Nadolny, has touched a nerve and a deep yearning of our time. Not only are the nerves of many of our contemporaries raw from constant stress. Our hectic lifestyle damages our souls and they suffer from the "relentless" pressure to save time. When everything has to keep going more quickly, when not a moment can be wasted at work, when there are no more breaks, when everything speeds up more and more, then we need an antidote: the discovery of slowness. There are many things we need to rediscover through slowness and quiet. Instead of speeding up we need to slow down.

If we watch a panther in a cage, we marvel at how majestic and slow its movements are. We know that in the very next moment it could pounce with lightning speed upon its prey. But it has time, it gives itself time. For us time is money. We must save as much time as possible, so that we have free time for more important things. But the question then is: what is more important for us? With the time we save we often cannot do very much. Usually we rush somewhere. But where? Our hectic attitude has taken us over. It even dominates our leisure. Here too we have to do as much as possible in the shortest possible time. But in this constant rushing about many people find they can no longer feel or experience much at all. They only feel alive amid a lot of hustle and bustle. But they no longer feel life itself. They no longer feel themselves, their breathing, their body, the stirrings of their heart. "Idleness is the beginning of all love," the poet Ingeborg Bachman once said.

We can practise this idling in our daily activities. Walk slowly, notice every step, do not let yourself be driven by anything. This keeps us wholly in the present and leads to intense experience and inner peace. Slowness has its own beauty. When a woman slowly strolls along the street, the men all look at her. She can allow herself to walk slowly. She enjoys her walk. The woman who trots briskly along does not want to be seen. She wants to get through the crowd as quickly as possible in order to get where she is going. She is not really there in the street, she is not in her body. She is directed only toward her goal and thereby loses the ability to feel herself, to enjoy herself. For Stoic philosophy, our life is a permanent celebration. We celebrate the fact that we are human beings with divine dignity. Something of this celebration can be felt in the slowness of our movements. We pick things up slowly, we walk slowly. We leave ourselves time for conversation. We leave ourselves time to eat. We eat slowly and with awareness. Then we notice how good the food tastes. We can enjoy it. We also celebrate when we chew a piece of bread really slowly.

The Angel of Slowness would like to introduce you to the art of *being*, living intensely. Try it some time at work, consciously walk more slowly when you are going from the door of one office to another. When you go out for a walk, try to feel every step you take, feel how you tread on the earth and lift your feet again. Try to pick up your cup slowly and hold it in your hand. In the evening undress slowly. Then you will find everything becomes a symbol, how putting aside your clothes comes to symbolize putting aside cares of the day. In the morning try to wash slowly, enjoy the cold water that refreshes you. Then get dressed slowly. The liturgy provides for this slow dressing. When the priest puts on the Mass vestments he says: "I put on the garments of salvation." Likewise, you can consciously be glad of the clothes you put on. You dress yourself in them and prepare to meet the day. You can

thank God in the words of Psalm 139: "I praise you because
you have formed me so wonderfully" (v. 14). So the Angel of
Slowness wants to lead you to live with attentive awareness
and teach you the art of making your life a permanent celebration.

37 The Angel of Retreat

In the fourth century there was a great movement of retreat by monks who had had enough of the noisiness of the world and were disappointed that the Church itself was becoming worldly. They retreated to the desert, in order to live alone apart from the world. There they wanted to contemplate the truth about themselves and follow their deepest desire, to experience God in prayer and become one with him. It was astonishing that it was precisely those who had retreated from the world who had such an unexpectedly strong effect on it. Crowds of pilgrims and people seeking help set out from Rome and Athens for the deserts of Egypt, in order to get advice from the Desert Fathers. They clearly felt that these men who had had the courage to retreat and to stand before God, just as they were, understood more about being human than philosophers and doctors who remained amid the hustle and bustle of the world.

From time to time each of us needs to retreat from the noise and rush of daily life. Otherwise it overwhelms us. We function but no longer really live, we are no longer ourselves. If you go to a silent place, it can happen that you take all the noise of your world with you, and it is not very pleasant to confront all the things that surface in you. It requires some time for you to free yourself from your everyday problems. This is when your inner retreat really begins. You withdraw, step back from what you are doing, what you are involved in. You get into touch with yourself. You discover what is going on in the depths of your heart. You discover your deepest truth. This is sometimes painful. But when you look at it and hold it out to God, who accepts you as you are, you feel an inner freedom and peace. You feel your uniqueness. You feel that you are valuable and important, because you can make a unique impression on this world, which no one else can. Perhaps then you discover the inner spring that bubbles inside you and never fails, because it is a divine spring, the spring of the Holy Ghost.

The Angel of Retreat would also like to give you the courage sometimes to retreat from your husband or wife or partner. If you are constantly with another person, you will feel trapped. You cling to each other. This is not good for either of you. You need space and freedom between you, so that each can breathe and bring his or her own special qualities to the relationship. Sometimes your wife or husband may bitterly reproach you for retreating. But I know many who have tried it. They have found that it has also benefited their life together. You become your whole self gain. It is like a health cure, in which you regain access to your own resources. Your life together regains its sparkle. You recover your imagination and enjoyment. You are prepared to do new things with your husband or wife, your boyfriend or girlfriend. If you retreat, you feel that you are not defined simply by your partner. You need something deeper, your own source of life, God who made you a unique human being. So my wish for you is that the Angel of Retreat may show you when it is time to retreat again. I wish that then you will find you are not alone, because the Angel of Retreat is with you, revealing a new horizon to your future life.

38 The Angel of Attentiveness

The Angel of Attentiveness is related to the Angel of Slowness. Today attentiveness is a favourite word used by spiritual writers. In particular the Vietnamese Buddhist monk Thich Nhat Hanh often speaks about attentiveness, the art of living attentively. For him this is the whole wisdom of Buddhism, to let the energy of attentiveness flow into every single daily activity. Even as a young monk he learned to perform all his everyday tasks attentively. His whole ascesis and daily training consisted in being attentive to everything, to his breathing, walking, washing dishes, washing his hands. Every time he washed his hands he said: "Water flows over these hands. I will use it carefully to preserve our precious planet."

The word attentiveness is related to respect, observe, esteem, notice. It is connected with being awake. If you pay attentive respect to your breathing, attentively measure your step, attentively pick up a spoon, if you are wholly involved in what you are doing at the moment, you are awake. Buddha is called the Awakened One. Many people may spend their whole life asleep. They do not notice what they are doing. They have illusions about their life. But they are not in touch with real life. Attentiveness should bring us into contact with things and people. A Zen monk was once asked about his practice of meditation. He answered: "When I eat, I am eating. When I sit, I am sitting. When I stand, I am standing. When I walk, I am walking." The questioner said: "There is nothing special about that. We all do it." The monk replied: "No, when you sit, you are already standing up and when you stand up, you are already on your way."

The practice of meditation consists simply in this, paying attention to what I am doing at the moment. Then I realize that attentiveness is a spiritual power, which gives my life a new spice. I have the feeling that I myself am living, instead of being lived. I feel that life is a mystery, full of depths, full of brightness, full of joy.

Attentiveness is connected with esteem, valuing things. I treat my breathing with respect, because in it I feel God's breath filling me with life, penetrating my whole body with its healing warmth. Respectfully, I pick up the tool I am going to use, because I see the care that has been put into making it. I treat the flowers in my room with respect, because in them I feel the mystery of creation and the Creator himself.

Not only for Zen monks, but also for Western monks, attentiveness is the sign of a spiritual person. St Benedict told his monks to treat the monastery's equipment and tools with care and respect, because everything is precious, everything is a sacred altar vessel. However, even we monks often forget to be attentive. Too often we go about our books unconsciously, use cutlery or handle tools without awareness. Too often we bang the door unconsciously. So in our daily unawareness and inattentiveness we all need the Angel of Attentiveness to keep in contact with us, wake us from our sleep and make us live attentively, wholly in the present moment, give all our attention to what we are doing at the time.

If I am attentive in everything I do, this adds sweetness to my life. I am wholly in the present, wholly at one with myself and things. But this attentiveness is not automatic. It has to be practised every day. It becomes the measure of my spirituality. However many pious words I speak, or however many spiritual talks I give, without attentiveness they are all hot air. My wish for you is that the Angel of Attentiveness may lead you ever deeper into the art of living, so that you discover the joy of living and do everything with attentiveness and respect, because everything is valuable, everything is wonderfully created by God and his Spirit.

39 The Angel of Mildness

For me the mild autumn light is like people who look mildly at themselves, their faults and weaknesses, but also at others and their human failings. With their mild gaze they bathe their own reality and that of others near them in a mild light. In the mild autumn light everything looks beautiful. Then the bright leaves on the tree shine in all their beauty. Even the withered tree is beautiful. Everything gets its own shine. I know old people who beam out a mildness of this kind. I like to be near them. I like talking to them. They make me feel that I can be as I am, and I agree: "Everything is good." Often life has buffeted these old people this way and that. They have had their ups and downs. But now in the autumn of their life they look at everything with a mild gaze. Nothing human is alien to them. They do not judge. They let it shine in the mild autumn light, just as it is.

The medieval word *mild* comes from "mill." So "mild" means milled or ground up fine, tender, soft, mellow. We are not mild by nature. Mildness requires the grinding process. Only then does the hard corn become soft and mealy. The word "mealy" comes from *mola*, millstone. Mild old people have been ground in the mill of life. They have been through crises, they have known despair. They have been through dark valleys. They have often battled with their faults and weaknesses and often lost the battle. But they have always stood up again and fought on. The millstone of their life has ground them soft. They have not rebelled against this millstone. They said yes to it grinding them up. So they have become mild. Perhaps you have experienced the angel described by Werner Bergengruen in his Angel Prayer:

Brother Angel, every night,
before the demons could undo me,
your guardian wings enfolded me
and roused pinkening morning light. . . .

You have borne me like a brother
through the fiery depths of hell.
On the cliff face sheer and tall
you cut out steps where feet might slither.

You've kept me safe from rope and bullet,
opened walls for me to pass.
However much I might repel it
nothing changed your faithfulness.

Though I did not thank or greet you,
Angel, now escort me home.
Through the dark and dismal street, you
Angel, snatch me out of time.

Wherever, Angel, it may be,
lead me once more. Then you are free.

From my breast remove the stone.
Angel, don't leave me alone.

Clearly the poet felt that the Angel of Mildness had carried him through all hells and abysses, ground him in the mill and made him mild.

Mildness and gentleness belong together. For the writer monk Evagrius Ponticus, gentleness is the mark of the spiritual person. Ascesis, which only makes you hard and self-righteous, is worthless. Only someone who is gentle like David and Jesus have understood the spiritual way. Those who judge other people harshly have not really overcome their own faults and weaknesses. They have only repressed them. They have fought against them violently, and now they attack others with the same violence. They project their repressed passions onto others. They have not been through the mill of truth. So they have never become soft and tender.

My wish for you is that you may meet many of these Angels of Mildness in your life. You will feel how people like this do you good. Perhaps you already know some of these mild people. Seek them out, talk to them, ask them how they became the way they are. Then you can learn from them how to look mildly and bathe your life in mild autumn light, which lends everything in you its own dignity and beauty, even your failures. When you have been to this school of the mild, perhaps you too will be able to become an Angel of Mildness for other people, who rage against themselves, judge themselves harshly, and despair at their own shortcomings. You do not need to say very much to them. Perhaps they will feel from your mild gaze that they too can see their life in another light, not in a harsh condemning light, but bathed in the mild soft light of autumn.

40 The Angel of Humility

Demut, the German word for "humble," comes from Old High German *diomuoti*, meaning "willing to serve." In Germanic knightly allegiance, "serving" meant being someone's servant or runner. This was how the old Germans or Teutons translated the Latin word *humilis*, meaning "lowly," from which the English word "humble" comes via Old French. For the Old Germans humility, *Demut*, meant having the courage to serve, to serve life, stand up for others, to run for others. It goes with the readiness to set yourself aside, to become free of yourself in order to risk yourself for others. This sense does not cover the whole of the biblical idea of humility, but just one aspect of it.

The Latin *humilitas* comes from *humus*, meaning earth, soil. *Humilitas* means the courage to accept our own earthiness, the courage to reconcile ourselves with the truth that we are from the earth, that we are flesh and blood people, with instincts and vital needs. Those who do not have this courage to look at the truth about themselves are blind. We are shown this in the famous story of the healing of the man born blind in John 9. This is a man who has been blind from birth. Clearly he had such a terrible childhood that all he could do was to shut his eyes to the reality of it. He created his own world in order to survive. He had replaced the negative images others had imposed on him with his own highly idealistic image. But this idealistic image did not accord with his own reality. So he had to close his eyes to it. Jesus heals him by spitting on the ground, the earth, *humus*, and mixing the spit with earth into a mud paste. He smears this dirt onto the blind man's eyes to tell him: "You are from the earth. Reconcile yourself with the dirt that is in you. Only then will you be able to see again. You need courage for the truth, for your humanity, your earthiness. Then you will be able to go through the world with your eyes open."

For monks humility, meaning the courage to face the truth about yourself, is the sign of genuine spirituality. If you are proud of your spiritual life and set yourself above others, who give way to their moods and instincts, you have not yet come face to face with the truth about yourself. Herman Hesse describes this in a fascinating way in his book *Siddharta*. At first Siddharta practises severe asceticism, then he fails. Then he goes out into the world and gives rein to all his desires. Finally, he becomes sated with this life and he returns. At the river he suddenly receives his great enlightenment. He sees the "child people" crossing the river in a boat. Earlier on he had set himself above them. Now he sympathizes with them. He feels a deep oneness with them. He is just like them. He feels compassion for them but also hope. He judges no one but he knows that for all people what counts is the greater love that can transform everything. The Angel of Humility has taken him into its school and taught him that he can experience oneness with other people and himself only if he is prepared to come down to them and to his own truth.

Humble people are not people who belittle themselves, who shirk all the things they should do, because they do not trust themselves. They are not creeps who demean themselves by false obsequiousness. But they are people who have the courage to face the truth about themselves, and so to behave modestly. They know that all this world's abysses are also in them. So they judge no one. Because they have bent down and faced their own earthiness, they can become Angels of Humility, who can set those who have failed on their feet again.

Humilitas is also connected with humour. Humble people are humorous. They can laugh about themselves. They can stand back and look at themselves calmly, because they have allowed themselves to be as they are, a human being of earth and heaven, a human being with faults and weaknesses, who is also valuable and lovable. My wish for you is that the Angel of Humility may give you the courage to accept and love yourself in your own earthiness and humanity. Then you will give out hope and confidence to everyone you meet. The Angel of Humility will create a space around you, in which people find the courage to step down into their own reality and thereby step up into true life.

41 The Angel of Fulfillment

The word fulfillment can have various meanings. We long for our wishes and desires to be fulfilled. We also know that no human being can fulfill our deepest yearnings. If we love someone we feel filled with this love. But at the same time the longing grows for an absolute love, absolute security, absolute support. No mortal human being can give us this absolute. From time immemorial, humans have called upon angels to help them when they wanted their desires to be fulfilled. They have felt that they could not fulfill everything by themselves. Of course we can fulfill our wish for a new dress or a new car, if we have enough money in the bank. But we need the Angel of Fulfillment to help us if we wish for a successful friendship, good health, a job that suits us. The fulfillment of these wishes depends on things beyond our control. Then we turn to our Angel and ask it to stand by us and grant our heart's desire.

To fulfill also means to do something and finish it. The Angel of Fulfillment will strengthen you to perform what you have undertaken. It does you no good if you only go halfway, if you only begin something and do not finish it. This goes for household repairs. Nothing is worse than a half-decorated room that is never finished. It goes for a letter to your friend that you have begun. A letter that is not finished just annoys you. Then you need the Angel of Fulfillment to give you the power and the perseverance to finish what you have started. Only then can you go on to the next job with new strength. Things you have begun but not finished discourage you. You cannot always live on bits and pieces. You long for something to be complete.

This is the next meaning of the word fulfill: completion.

The Greek word for completion is *telos*. It means goal, whole, completion, perfection. John's Gospel frequently uses this word for the love of Jesus Christ. "Having loved his own who were in the world, he loved them to the end" (John 13:1). As he is dying on the cross he says: "It is finished" (John 19:39). This saying recalls the sentence with which the mystery cults concluded their sacred ceremonies. Here completion means initiation into God's mystery. God alone is complete and perfect. When we say people have lived a full life, that they are fulfilled and complete, we also mean that they share in God's fullness, in the completion that God alone can give. The Angel of Fulfillment would like to lead you into the mystery of completion and thereby into the mystery of God. In everything you complete there shines something of the completion that is in God. You get an inkling of your life becoming whole. Sometimes, perhaps you have the impression that your life consists of many bits and pieces, which you have not put together. The Jewish mystics interpreted their own suffering with the expression: "Only a broken heart is a whole heart." The Angel of Fulfillment wants to show you that the many bits and pieces of your life fit together, that they make up a complete whole. Your life can become whole and healthy, fulfilled and complete. You are no longer torn hither and thither by contradictory wishes and needs. You are whole. You are fulfilled. The Angel of Fulfillment brings back together what is torn apart in you and completes what is in fragments. It fulfills your deepest yearning to be one, to be whole.

42 The Angel of Endurance

At the beginning of a year or a week or even a day, many people plan to do something. They are enthusiastic about a book they have read. Accordingly, they want to change their life at once. Or they have heard a lecture about how they can manage their time better, or work on their faults. So they set to work with a will. But after a short while they run out of steam. It becomes too difficult and they give up. All at once it is no longer any fun to work on yourself, particularly when you are not seeing any results. So there is no point. You know you won't get anywhere. But by giving up the plan you are giving up a bit of yourself. You no longer trust yourself. You resign. So gradually a sense of meaninglessness slips in. Everything is meaningless. Nothing changes. I cannot alter myself. I cannot make myself any better. Poemen, one of the early Fathers, said to a young monk who was filled with such thoughts of resigning: "What is the point of applying yourself to a craft and not learning it properly?" Learn the craft of becoming a human being and stop moaning!

The Angel of Endurance would like to lead you to stick at what you have undertaken to do. As the proverb says: "The road to hell is paved with good intentions." If you keep planning to do something and never carry it through, you are preparing a hell for yourself here and now. Your life will become a hell of self-reproaches and self-criticism, which will torment you. Without endurance your life has no constancy. The word endure comes from *durare*, meaning to last, to remain, to be constant, to stick it out. If you go to work without endurance you never stand firm. You flap around, you nibble at things. But nothing develops. Something can grow only if it can take root. Jesus himself compares such people without endurance to the stony ground on which the word of God falls: "They have no root in themselves, but endure for a while; then when trouble or persecution arises . . . immediately they fall away" (Mark 4:17). As soon as things get difficult, as soon as they feel any resistance, they give up. Gradually this makes them not trust themselves any longer.

Consider when you are next going to need the Angel of Endurance. Perhaps it is at work, where not everything is going as you would wish. If you stick at it, if you do not give up, when you do not just tell yourself there is nothing to be done, you will see that the situation at your work place can change. Or perhaps you are working on one of your weaknesses. You think you have so often planned to learn to control your anger or deal with your eating problem. But nothing has worked. First you must set yourself realistic goals and not chase after illusions. You must see what you really can change and what is simply your character, with which you must come to terms. But when you undertake to change something in yourself, you must stick at it. If you do not succeed, you must ask yourself whether you went about it in the wrong way or took on too much. Then set yourself a more modest goal. But stick at it, and you will find your endurance is rewarded. The Angel of Endurance will give you the feeling: it is possible to change something in myself; it is enjoyable if I stick at it with endurance. I am not simply a prey to circumstances. I can do something. Trust that you are not alone. When you want to give in, look about you! Then you will see the Angel of Endurance standing beside you. The Angel will not leave you until your life acquires a firm foundation, one that is constant and enduring.

43 The Angel of Trust

I constantly hear people complaining, "I can't trust anyone. I did not learn trust as a child. My trust has so often been abused. So with the best will in the world I can't manage to trust anyone." People like this are lonely and remain so. They do not trust themselves to go out to another person, because they are afraid of being let down again. Neither do they trust another person's love. Immediately doubt comes: "He only loves me because he is sorry for me, or because he wants something from me, or wants to use me for his own ends." It does not help such people if I say to them: "You just have to trust people!" They want to trust people, but they can't. The reason usually lies in their childhood. They had no choice about it. On the other hand, those who experienced their parents as reliable trust not only their parents. They also approach other people with trust. They have a basic trust in life, in things, in God, so they can be daring. They take risks because they trust that things will be all right.

If I wish you the Angel of Trust, I trust you are not at the mercy of the mistrust you acquired as a child. You can learn to trust. You can go to school with the Angel of Trust. You can't just decide that from today on you will trust people. Trust has to grow. You need some positive experiences of other people, people who prove themselves to be reliable and trustworthy. But you also need to be prepared to trust the trustworthiness that people offer you. If you regard your friends with distrust, they have no chance to prove you can trust them. You will take everything they say and do in a negative way. But you must be prepared to give it a try. How do you do this? You can behave as if they are worthy of trust. You can see how it goes if you take everything your friends say as genuine, if you take it all on trust. Of course a few doubts will still slip in. But you must reserve these doubts for later. Just try for once to trust your friends for at least a week. You will see how this does you good, and how it proves increasingly right to trust them.

Of course there is always a risk when you trust someone. You have no guarantee that your trust is justified. It helps me to know that I am supported at a deeper level. I know I am supported by a higher power. Even if a human being does abuse my trust, I trust God, who holds me in his loving hands. This trust in God prevents me from falling into a slough of despond if someone abuses my trust.

From time immemorial people have trusted that an angel is beside them. They have called upon these guardian angels, not only in the midst of dangerous traffic, but also when they they were in doubt whether to trust someone else. My wish for you is that you may know that you are accompanied by the Angel of Trust. Then you do not have to be 100 per cent certain whether you can trust this or that person. You do not lose your trust even if someone disappoints you. The Angel of Trust will stay with you and keep renewing your courage to trust yourself and risk trusting others. This is what trust means, relying on something over which you do not have power.

Because daring is an essential part of trust, it is good to know that an Angel of Trust is beside me. The Angel has contact with what is beyond my power. At a deeper level, it gives me the trust that I need in my dealings with people. It gives me the trust that can never be completely destroyed by other people, because that is not within their power either.

This trust gives me freedom to keep going back to people with trust. It makes me able to be daring, to take risks. "Who dares wins," says the proverb. If you want to control everything beforehand, even if you succeed, you will let life slip between your fingers. The Angel of Trust wants to lead you

to put more and more trust in life and other people. You will
see that you are not determined by the lack of trust you learnt
as a child. An Angel wants to set your trust on a firmer foundation, upon which you can build your life.

44 The Angel of Compassion

Compassionate people are those who have a heart for the poor, the orphaned, the unfortunate, the lonely. But before they can have a heart for the poor, they must first have a heart for what is poor and unhappy in themselves. We must learn first to be compassionate with ourselves. The Latin *misericordia* means mercy or compassion, having a heart for the unhappy and unfortunate. When the Jews speak of mercy or compassion, they think of the mother's womb. The merciful God carries us lovingly in the womb. Like a mother he can wait until we grow up to fit the image he has made of us. When Jesus has compassion for people, the Bible often uses the Greek word *splanchnizomai*. It means "to be gripped in the guts." For the Greeks the guts or intestines were the seat of sensitive feelings. So to be compassionate means letting someone else touch the place where I am sensitive. The Bible has yet another word for mercy or compassion: *eleos*, meaning tenderness, sympathy, pity.

So being compassionate toward myself means treating myself tenderly, not raging against myself, not making too many demands on myself, but simply having a heart for myself, just as I now am, having a heart for what is weak and orphaned in myself. We often treat ourselves pitilessly. We judge ourselves when we make a mistake. We scold ourselves if something goes wrong. We have a ruthless judge inside ourselves, a hardhearted superego, who judges all our thoughts and feelings, who punishes us if we do not correspond with its demands. We often cannot cope with this ruthless superego. We need the words of Jesus, who shows us the merciful Father who does not reject the prodigal son but makes a feast for him, because he who was lost has been found, he who was dead has returned to life. We need an Angel of Compassion to take the power away from our inner judge and fill our heart with compassionate love. It is not enough to decide to be compassionate with your mind and will. A ruthless superego lodges in our unconscious. In order to overcome it we need the Angel of Compassion in us.

When we treat ourselves with compassion, then we can also learn compassion toward others. I know many people who are compassionate toward the sick and lonely, but who are completely ruthless toward themselves. There is a place in their heart for everyone else but none for themselves. They force themselves to repress all their own needs, in order to be there for others. But this lack of compassion for myself will distort the help I give to others. A kind of possessiveness will slip into my love. I will get annoyed if my too great love is not honoured. In order to love another person from the heart, in order really to have a heart for him or her, I must first get in touch with my own heart, I must feel with my heart for all that is poor and unhappy in myself. Then I can be compassionate. Then I will not condemn others, but I will embrace them, together with all that is unhappy, broken, unattractive in my heart. Then my help will not give them a bad conscience. They will find a place, a home in my heart. My wish for you is that the Angel of Compassion will teach you to open your heart to what is poor in yourself and others. Then your heart will become like a womb, in which you yourself and others can grow. People around you will also be able to get in touch with their own heart and cease condemning themselves ruthlessly. "Anyone who has a heart can be saved," says one of the fourth-century Church Fathers. If you have a heart for the poor and weak, your life will succeed. Then the Angel in you will rejoice over the compassion that dwells in your heart.

45 The Angel of Comfort

We need comfort if we have experienced a loss, if a friendship has broken up, if someone has hurt us deeply, if someone we love has died. A look at language will show us how the experience of comfort can differ. *Trost*, the German word for comfort, is related to the English "trust" and to *Treue*, meaning truth or faithfulness. So it is connected with steadfastness. Those who have suffered a loss, lose their balance. They need someone to restore their strength, their steadfastness. The Greek Bible's word for comfort is *parakalein*. It means to summon, invite, appeal for help, encourage, comfort, speak words of consolation. Those experiencing a lack or loss need an angel to stand beside them, to hold them when necessary, and speak words of comfort. For the Greeks comforting consists primarily in speaking, offering words that restore meaning to the sense of meaninglessness that strikes at first with every loss. But the words must not be mere platitudes, because these will not reach the other person. If I speak platitudes, I am not really speaking to the other person but at him. I say something or other of which I am not even convinced myself. I utter words which give no support, make no sense of the loss. Comforting means really speaking to the other person, saying words that reach her, that are valid for her personally, that go to her heart. Comforting means finding words from heart to heart, words that come from my heart, not hackneyed empty phrases, words that touch the other person's heart, that open up a new horizon for him or her and offer some firm ground to stand on.

The Latin word for comfort is *consolari*. Ultimately, it means being with people who are alone, who have been left alone with their pain, their loss, their need. So to comfort or console means getting inside those who are locked up in themselves, whose need has closed their mouth and heart. Not everyone can do this. Not everyone has the courage to knock at the door of those who have barricaded themselves in with their pain. Not everyone has the courage to go into a house of mourning and meet the mourner's bottomless need and loneliness. Being with sufferers also means sharing their pain, staying with them in their pain. I cannot console them from the outside, by mouthing pious words I have read somewhere else. I have to get inside them. I must enter their house of darkness, destruction and suffering. If you are able to go into a house of mourning, the mourner will experience you as an Angel of Comfort. He will feel that in you the angel of God has visited him like a "dawning from on high" (Luke 1:78).

From time immemorial people have appealed to the Angel of Comfort in their pain, to visit them and stay with them. In his tenor aria for his Michaelmas cantata, Johann Sebastian Bach expresses it thus: "Stay, you Angels, stay with me! Hold me up on either side, so that my footsteps do not slide!" It is a fervent song, which trusts that we shall not be left alone with our suffering, but that God's angels will accompany us and stay with us and be there until our pain is transformed into a song of thanksgiving. My wish for you is that an Angel may comfort you in your sadness. May this Angel set you firmly on your feet again if you are stumbling, may it speak to you with consoling words when you have become speechless with pain, may it visit you in your loneliness and give you the feeling you are no longer alone, because an Angel is standing beside you who will go with you all the way. If you know about the Angel of Comfort, you will be able to face your sadness and be comforted. You must not just ignore your sadness. When your sadness is consoled it will no longer weaken you but lead you deep into the mystery of your own self and the mystery of Jesus Christ, who has come down into our sadness as the "whole world's comfort."

46 The Angel of Prudence

Prudence is the first of the four cardinal virtues. It is the capacity to discover what is appropriate and beneficial for me here and now. The Latin word *prudentia* comes from *providentia* and means foresight, caution. Prudent people look out. They behave with circumspection. They see beyond what is under their noses. They have a wider horizon. They discern reality and see things as they are. For the Greek philosopher Aristotle, prudence is the precondition for all the other virtues. First of all, I need to see reality correctly. Then I can behave appropriately, According to Josef Pieper, this virtue makes people "fit to be and to do what they are actually at." My life will only be fitting if I behave in accordance with its reality. The ancients distinguished prudence from wisdom. Wisdom knows the mystery of being, whereas prudence sees how to apply this knowledge of reality to each moment and convert it into practical living.

You need the Angel of Prudence when you have to make a decision. The Angel of Prudence sees further than you. It has a wider horizon. It foresees (*providentia*) what consequences your decision might have. You must ask your Angel of Prudence to help you discern the deepest motives for your decisions and which decision fits the reality best. You need the Angel of Prudence if you have to judge a situation. You are asked to sort out a dispute. Over-eagerly, many people think all they need is love. Then everything will resolve itself. Prudent people see the situation clearly. They seek for the causes of the conflict. They listen to different opinions. Only when they have heard it all and thought it over do they give a judgment, one that seeks for ways to settle the dispute. The prudent person sees everything and tries to understand everything in order to be able to judge rightly.

Jesus calls prudent those who have built their house upon a rock. They do not behave with undue haste. They do not build their house on the sand of their illusions, or the sand of their enthusiasm but on the rock of a solid life, as Jesus preached in his Sermon on the Mount. Prudent people weigh everything up. They act with consideration. They know what is at stake. Prudent people are not know-alls but they know the essential and think about it carefully. Jesus praises the prudence of the unjust steward, who finds the right solution to a difficult situation. In a tight spot he realizes what he can do about his guilt, so that he does not lose his self-respect. The prudent person finds the solution appropriate to the moment. The prudent virgins look ahead. They look beyond the moment and think of the future. The foolish virgins live only for the moment. Prudence is clearly necessary for our life to succeed.

In German prudence is often connected with craftiness. But this is not what it means. *Klug,* the German world for prudence, actually means: fine, tender, delicate, cultured, intellectually agile, courageous, brave. Prudent people think not only with their mind but also with their heart. They bravely seize the opportunity that is offered them. They see the fine distinctions, which cruder minds would overlook. Prudence is practical reason, knowledge converted into action, in accordance with the reality. Knowing much helps little if you do not know what is right for this moment. I wish you the Angel of Prudence, so that at every moment you know which way to go. May this Angel take you further and lead you into greater freedom, breadth, and love.

47 The Angel of Reverence

The idea of reverence combines honour and fear. In this case the fear is not fear of other people or dangerous situations, but awe. It means not pushing yourself forward but keeping the appropriate distance. Reverence is a religious feeling. "It is the sense of the unapproachably holy, which in earlier consciousness surrounded everything that was high, mighty, and glorious" (Romano Guardini). Those who are reverent do not take possession of what they marvel at. They stand back in awe. They show the necessary respect for other people, creation, the marvellous. They do not insist on penetrating a person's mystery. They let the mystery be. Romano Guardini holds that all true culture begins with people standing back, allowing others their dignity and work its beauty. True culture requires reverence. In all religions angels give people the feeling of reverence. They bring something from beyond into people's lives, something that kindles them, something that transcends them, from which they can only stand back in awe.

Out of reverence, I curb my curiosity about people and do not probe their intimate secrets. Ultimately, for St Benedict, reverence for other people means believing in their good core and seeing the divine spark, Christ himself, in them. I don't just see other people's faults and weaknesses; I look deeper. Behind their sometimes unimpressive facade, I see their real yearnings. In the depths of their heart all people want to be good. I do not deny the wrong that I see them do. But I do not condemn them. I try to look behind the scene of the wrongdoing. I realize that no one does wrong for pleasure, but always out of despair, as Albert Görres, the Munich psychiatrist, once said.

Reverence has to do with respect. I do not respect people

124

because of what they do but because they are human beings. If people feel respected they take heart. They rediscover their divine dignity. Today I still remember what an Argentinian friend said about my father: "He makes you feel respected." In a strange country, this meant a lot to him, not to be branded a foreigner but to be respected as a human being. Reverence respects the boundaries the other person wants to see maintained. It respects people's intimacy. We need such Angels of Reverence today at a time when there is a hunger for sensational intimate details about people's private lives. Reverence creates an atmosphere of delicacy and protectiveness, tenderness and respect, which does us good. With it we really feel like human beings with unencroachable dignity.

Reverence has to do with greatness. Today there is an urge to drag what is supposedly great in the dirt. The inferior cannot bear the fact that there is genuine human greatness. They have to spy out its weaknesses, prove to themselves that there cannot be such a thing as human greatness, in order to justify their own mediocrity. Reverence acknowledges greatness and rejoices in it. By rejoicing in it, I myself share in the greatness of what I admire. However, reverence is not only for the great but also for the little, the defenceless, the injured. This reverence recognizes their divine dignity, which also shines in the disfigured face of the tortured. Anyone who exploits another's defencelessness is shameless. He humiliates this human being. Reverence does the opposite. It gives people space and freedom to discover their own dignity and take heart.

Today on many occasions we need Angels of Reverence, to change the climate of cynicism and hunger for sensation into one of respect for human dignity. If such an Angel of Reverence went to a party, gossip about other people would stop, an atmosphere of respect would arise, in which all could be themselves, all would know they were respected. If such an Angel of Reverence turned up at the Town Hall and entered the debate in the Council Chamber, the cruel accusations hurled at members of the opposite party would cease. They would be ruled out of order. If such an Angel of Reverence joined a community, it would curb the curiosity that tried to pokes its nose into everyone else's secrets. Then we would not keep trying to change people. We would see each of them as a person and respect them for what they are. People can only change themselves in an atmosphere of reverence and respect, in which they do not lose their own self-respect. Because they know their own dignity as persons, they can change, grow to be more like the person that corresponds to their divine dignity.

My wish for you is that you may live near many Angels of Reverence. Then your feeling for the deep mystery that is in you will grow. You will experience what being human means. You will enjoy your own humanity. I also wish that you may become an Angel of Reverence for others and learn to see your neighbours with the eyes of an Angel of Reverence. Then you will give others space in which to be wholly themselves.

48 The Angel of Understanding

Psychology tries to heal sick people by understanding them without criticizing them, without judging them, without condemning them, whatever they may tell you. If people feel understood they can express everything that is inside them. They no longer anxiously try to hide things. They feel that with this listener everything is in good hands, this listener understands me, and thus enables me to understand myself better. Someone who understands me, without judging or condemning me, has a healing and liberating effect on me. At last I can talk about what has been distressing me for so long, something I have always held back because I was ashamed of it, because it goes against my moral principles. When I speak about it openly to someone else it loses its poisonous effect. I no longer need to use all my energy to hide this unpleasant and unmentionable thing. It comes out of hiding into the light, so it can change.

The word understand comes from "stand." The German for "understand" is *verstehen*, which also comes from *stehen*, meaning "stand." However, in German the prefix is different. Instead of "under-", as in English, it is *ver-*, which is related to the Latin *pro* (for), *prae* (before), and *per* (through). Those who "forestand" (*verstehen*) me, stand before me, in front of me, and protect me from the projections others cast upon me. They stand before me, in front of me, so that behind them I can learn to stand myself. They stand for me, so that I can stand for myself. They stand by me, so that I can stand by myself better, so that I can get a better standing. They stand with me through my problems. They do not wobble when they hear about my weaknesses. By standing my situation, they also make me able to stand my life, to stand it with staying power. I no longer stumble about because I don't know what is the matter with me. I can stand by myself, because someone else understands me, and this understanding is a standby, a support for me.

We say of two friends that they understand each other blindly. I don't just want a friend who understands me, but also a friend with whom I understand myself. People who understand each other blindly, who don't have constant misunderstandings, stand on good terms with each other. They stand well with each other. They stand together. Each allows the other his or her own stand. You do not have to take it from me. You can be as you are. You can do as you feel. You do not have to adapt your stand to mine. Understanding each other means that neither of us exploits the other for our own ends, but we both stand well with each other, we stand in a good relation to one another. However, this succeeds only when we can both stand well for ourselves. I can have a good understanding with a friend only if I understand myself, if I have gained enough self-knowledge. If I can stand only when the other person is with me, I am dependent. That is against my dignity. In order to understand myself, I need the Angel of Understanding. It understands me better than I do myself. It sees things in me that are still hidden from me or that I do not want to see. It sees them without judging me. It sees and understands. This enables me to see myself as I am, understand myself, and take responsibility for myself.

Understanding heals. In a pastoral conversation I am always pleased when the other person feels understood. Then there is a feeling of closeness and intensity. Then the other person can take heart, be heartened. Because you feel understood, you stand again. You can breathe again. You lose your fear that you are not good enough, that you should not be as you are. You feel firm ground under your feet again. So my wish for you is that you should meet many Angels of Understanding, who give you new standing power. I also wish that you may become such an Angel of Understanding for others. You will experience how much good it does you if another person tells you: "I feel understood by you. I like being with you. It is good to stand with you. You stand in front of me. Then other people's prejudices do not get to me. I do not have to condemn myself. With you I can stand by myself."

49 The Angel of Darkness

If I wish you the Angel of Darkness, I am not wishing that everything around you and in you should become dark. What I am asking for is that an Angel should visit you and accompany you in your darkness. Sometimes it is dark in us. Our mood suddenly darkens, often we do not know where these dark feelings come from. If we look at a relationship or our marriage, it is as if we were standing in a dark cloud. Everything is threatening. We are afraid we will never find our way out of the darkness. If faith used to be a light to you on your way, it can happen that suddenly your faith also goes dark, that God hides behind the darkness in your heart.

Many people today suffer from depressive feelings. In depression everything becomes dark. Everything that used to give you joy slips away. You feel you are sitting in a dark hole and you can't get out. In this hole you can't even feel yourself. Everything becomes numb, meaningless, and dark. The light of human love no longer reaches you. Well-meant words just go over your head. Loving words sound empty. Words of advice go unheeded and have no effect. I hear the words, but I don't understand them. They do not reach me. Many who try to help someone out of a dark hole find they are powerless to do anything. So an Angel must come and climb down into this darkness and reach out its hand to these sufferers in their dark night. Such an Angel must not be afraid of the dark. It must be confident that it will not fall into a black abyss but that it has support. It needs courage to climb down into the dark hole, and sit with those who are down there in it.

The Angel of Darkness is also the Angel of Night. It is the angel who speaks to us in dreams. "At night I'll speak with the angel, if he acknowledges my eyes," writes Rilke in a poem.

If we don't know anything any more, if other people's words no longer reach us, often a dream like this can bring about a turning-point. All at once our spirits become lighter. I once accompanied a young woman who had been raped. Nothing I said reached her. All I could do was listen to her pain and distress and dry her tears. Then she dreamed of a cheeky child who was teasing a giant. Suddenly everything changed. For the first time she felt hope again. For the first time she felt alive again, and she recovered her will to live. What all my words failed to do, the Angel of Night accomplished through a dream. In the Bible God often sends his Angel to tell people something in a dream, to show them a new way and give them the certainty that God is with them and their life will succeed. Joseph sat in the deep pit with no hope of being saved. But he had been given the certainty in a dream that his life would succeed. The dream brought light into the darkness of the pit. So he did not give up, he hung on to the promise the Angel had given him in his dream. My wish for you is that the Angel of Night will visit you and show you your next step in a dream, to lead you out of darkness and on to the road of freedom and love.

50 The Angel of Quiet

Angels are delicate creatures. You can't grab hold of them. They come unexpectedly. You must lay yourself open so that you can meet them. Angels come soft-footed. You need to be very quiet in order to perceive them. There is an Angel who would like to teach you the art of silence, in the healing atmosphere of quiet. In our noisy world we need a lot of quiet, in order to recuperate. Kierkegaard famously said that if he were a doctor he would advise people: "Create silence!" Rabindranath Tagore invites us: "Bathe your soul in silence." Quiet is medicine for the soul, which is often clogged by the noise of the world. It can no longer breathe because noisy thoughts and images keep pressing in on it.

Everything great requires quiet in order to be born in us. "Only in silence can genuine knowledge be attained," says Romano Guardini. And Johannes Climacus, a monk in the early Church, says, "Silence is a fruit of wisdom and possesses the knowledge of all things." Silence prepares us to listen well, to hear the nuances in what someone says to us. Silence is necessary in order to hear God's voice in our hearts. Many people complain today that they do not experience God, that God has become a stranger to them. But they are so full of noise that they do not hear the still small impulses through which God speaks in their heart. We always have something to do. As soon as a delicate impulse touches us we shove it aside and turn back to what we can get hold of. So we never hear God's voice.

Stille, the German word meaning quiet, comes from *stillen*, meaning to suckle, quieten, put to rest. The mother suckles the hungry baby, so that it stops yelling. The Angel of Quiet wants to silence our noisy thoughts, our crying wishes and needs, so that we discover the quiet place in us. The mystics are convinced that there is a quiet place in each of us, where thoughts and feelings, wishes and needs have no access. It is also the place where people, with their expectations and demands, judgments and condemnations have no access. It is the place in me where I am wholly myself. It is the quiet place, where God himself dwells in me. There no one can harm me. There I am safe and sound. Every day I need to sit and meditate. In meditation I imagine how my breath and the word which I connect with my breath lead me into this inner quiet place. The people who come into my office today have no access to that place. There no one can reach me with their wishes, judgments, and condemnations. There I can breathe freely. There I am alone with my God. This gives my life dignity. In this inner quiet place I come into contact with my true self. Quiet changes me, as it changed the quarrelsome wife of Rabbi Sussja. It was said of her: "From that moment on she became quiet. When she became quiet she became happy. When she became happy she became good."

Especially if you have a lot to do with other people, if many people want something from you, if you get into intense conversations with them, you need the Angel of Quiet, to silence the countless words in your head that you hear every day. In silence you can draw breath again. You can off-load everything that other people have put onto you. The Angel of Quiet would like to lead you into the inner place, where not even the people for whom you are there can enter. Only if you are in contact with this inner quiet place can you get involved with others without fear. Then you need not be afraid that other people's problems will take you over and demand too much, or that you will be smeared by the dirt you are often dealing with in conversation.

There is a place where you remain untouched by all the rubbish people want to dump on you. In this inner quiet place you remain safe and sound. The Angel of Quiet would like to accompany you and keep reminding you that this place is already there in you. You do not have to create it. You need only get into touch with the quiet that is in you and can help you. There in the place of silence you can rest. There you are safe and sound. There there is something clear and pure in you, which cannot be troubled by the world's noise.

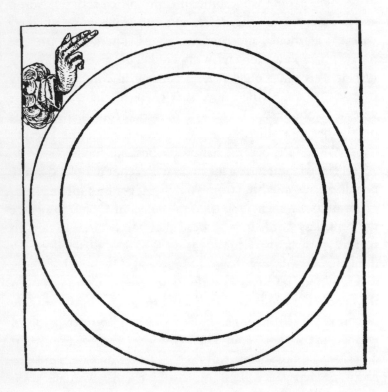

About the Author

Anselm Gruen is a monk of the Benedictine Abbey of Münsterschwarzach near Würzburg in southern Germany. He is an extremely popular religious writer with a number of best-selling books on the market in a number of languages. His highly original yet practical approach to theology combines his profound knowledge of both re-  ligion and psychology with special reference to C. G. Jung, the founder of Analytical Psychology. Fr Gruen writes books in order to help people by encouraging them really to "live their lives." This means looking for God in themselves, making something of themselves, and changing the way they are and behave.

Anselm Gruen was born in Junkerhausen in the Rhön area of Germany, where his family, originally from Munich, was evacuated during the Second World War. He grew up in Munich. In 1964 he took his school-leaving examination at the boarding school where he was educated and in the same year decided to become a Benedictine monk.

He studied theology from 1965 to 1971 at Saint Ottilien and in Rome. He wrote his doctoral thesis on Karl Rahner's theology and concept of salvation. He obtained his final qualification as a teacher at university and further education level in 1974. He then studied economics and financial management until 1976. The following year he was appointed adminstrator of the abbey of Münsterschwarzach, where he also directs residential courses in meditation techniques, psychoanalytical interpretation of dreams, fasting, and contemplation.

The abbey was founded in 815 and closed in 1803 but re-opened in 1913. It runs twenty flourishing trades and businesses, including a publishing house, a printshop, a goldsmith's, and a bookshop, all of which contribute to the monastery's finances. As a result, the abbey is largely self-supporting, and voluntary contributions are devoted to missionary work.